PR MATTERS: A Survival Guide for Church Communicators

ISBN: 0692862676
ISBN-13: 978-0692862674

Library of Congress Control Number: 2017909376

First Edition: 2017

For more information please visit the author's website at justinjdean.com
For bulk orders please visit churchprbook.com

Author Photo: Heidi Dean
Cover Design: Xavier Jones

WHAT OTHERS ARE SAYING

"In many churches, communication is completed by volunteers or paid staff that believe they can do in the church world what is done in the business world. The Church is not a business, so this thinking is a mistake. Having led both churches and companies, church communication is a different animal in a totally different world. Justin's book helps provide insight needed to be successful in the church world.

There are probably only a handful of people in the world with Justin Dean's experience of overseeing 582k Twitter followers, 320k Facebook followers, 250k weekly website visitors, and 100k weekly podcasters. The hard lessons he has learned and put into this book are a blessing. I urge all pastors and church leaders to read this book."

- Sutton Turner (@suttonturner),
Former Executive Elder & Executive Pastor, Mars Hill Church

"Justin knows communication. He not only led communication through one of the most difficult moments in the church in the last 20 years, but he has coached leaders in great seasons as well. If you want to understand church communications, you need to listen to Justin Dean."

- Carey Nieuwhof (@cnieuwhof),
Best-Selling Author and Founding Pastor of Connexus Church

"By far; the most-current, most-relevant read for anyone wanting their church to weather a crap storm. Oh look! The clouds are on the horizon. This book is your umbrella."

- Mark MacDonald (@markmac1023),
Strategic Communication Catalyst, Florida Baptist Convention
Best-Selling Author, *Be Known For Something*

"Justin is a church communications practitioner at heart, and *PR Matters* gets right to the point with practical tips that will help your church—no matter the size. I'm so glad he has chosen to share so many valuable insights in this book, so that other churches can learn from his many years of experiences."

- **Dave Adamson (@aussiedave),**
Social Media & Online Pastor, North Point Ministries

"Justin has a big heart for helping churches communicate better. Which is admirable considering what he has gone through. *PR Matters* is full of practical advice that your church can't afford to ignore."

- **Tim Schraeder (@timschraeder),**
Church Communications Specialist

"Too many churches don't realize the importance of PR until it's too late. Other churches have simply delegated control of their PR to people who don't understand the importance, or the ways in which it is changing.

Every church will learn from Justin's deep understanding and background in PR. Make *PR Matters* the one book your church leadership reads this year. The practical knowledge they will walk away with is truly priceless and will transform your church's communications."

- **Justin Brackett (@justinthesouth),**
Digital Communications Director, Seacoast Church

Read more at churchprbook.com

#PRMATTERS
Contents

DEDICATION

To all church communicators serving in the trenches, in a role
that no one understands or appreciates.
I'm with you, and I'm for you.

To Heidi. For bearing more than your share of the burden, but
always making it seem like we're serving together. I love you.

INTRODUCTION

I wrote this book for church communicators. People in the trenches and on the frontline, managing social media accounts and blogs and websites, and helping reach the world with the message of their church - the gospel of Jesus Christ.

Maybe you're a communications manager at a big church in Texas. Or a social media manager at a small church in Ohio. The media probably leaves you alone. You can make an innocent joke from stage and not worry about people freaking out. You can hold strong biblical beliefs on controversial topics and not get your windows smashed in. Your church is growing. Everyone loves your pastor. It's all sunshine and lollipops.

Now put yourself in my shoes for a minute. I was head of communications & public relations for a large conservative church in one of the most liberal areas in America, with one of the heaviest populations of unchurched people - Seattle, Washington.

Have you ever been to Seattle? There's no sunshine.

And lollipops are made of high fructose corn syrup, so definitely none of those in Seattle either. Unless it's a sugar-free, gluten-free, free-range, locally-sourced peace-pop.

You think I'm kidding?

I've been in the trenches just like you. I call them trenches, because we are in a very real war, whether you realize it yet or not. The rest of America may not be like hostile Seattle right now, but it's headed there fast. And it's happening so subtly and covertly that it's going to sneak up on you. You're probably already embracing it and you don't even realize it. I fear that you and your church are not going to be prepared. You may feel safe now. But it's going to get tough, and I fear that in order to survive, you'll adapt to the world around you rather than stand up to lead it.

I'm not saying we were the only ones who had it rough. I'm sure you've seen persecution and experienced trials as a church and as a Christian. If you haven't then you're doing something wrong. I'm not trying to say it's easy everywhere other than Seattle. I'm just saying there is nothing really like it, and the rest of world is quickly catching up. Try all you might to top my stories, but you'll fail.

It was tough enough trying to do ministry in a place that is always wet, dark, and depressing. But the people we were trying to reach in Seattle were inherently averse to Christianity. They were very active in stopping any kind of biblical preaching from occurring in their city, where ironically you can be anyone you want to be and do whatever you want to do, except preach the gospel. We constantly took hits at our church, but for many years we grew at an incredible pace, which can only be attributed to God's grace.

Until one day we took one hit too many, and it knocked us down. We couldn't rebuild fast enough to hold off the next hit, and we weren't prepared to weather so many storms at once.

You might be prepared for a hypothetical storm or two at your church, but are you prepared for a big one? When we got hit with a little extra pressure, we buckled. Things imploded. We weren't prepared.

The truth is we were too naive and maybe a little too arrogant to think we could sink. We didn't have a plan because we didn't think we needed one. As many times as I saw Titanic in the theaters, you'd think we would have known better, but we didn't.

I don't want your church to suffer the same fate that we did. We ultimately closed our doors for good because we had no other choice. There isn't anything I wouldn't give to get back to where we were, on the forefront of a resurgence. Leaders in a movement with a platform that had incredible influence and potential - and we were just getting started.

I want to help you grow the platform God has given you, and help prepare you to protect and defend it so you aren't ever forced to give it up. That's the goal of this book - to prepare you.

You may think that what happened to us will never happen to you. I pray it never does. But every month I talk with churches who are one step away from a fatal blow because they have no plan. Every year a new megachurch loses a pastor, and the whole world sees them fumble through how to communicate about it while still trying to love and serve their people well.

My desire is that within these pages you'll find practical help and hope for your church. I'm not a public relations expert or a communications guru. I'm nobody. Google my name and you'll wonder why anyone would buy a book by this guy, especially one about church PR.

But if you've read this far then you know there's something to learn, and that's all I want for you. That you'll be able to learn from my experiences and be able to apply the things I'm going to teach you so that your church can not only avoid the mistakes I've made, but that you'll be able to reach more people than ever with the message of the gospel.

Because the message we have, the story we have to tell, it's too important. You owe it to yourself, and to the people you are trying to reach, to make sure you are in the best position to effectively and consistently reach the most people.

Perhaps in the role you're in you feel like it's not up to you. You don't make the decisions, you just do as you're told. Maybe no one even understands what your role is, or how important it is. You might be a volunteer and don't feel empowered. Or if you're on staff, I'm sure you're underpaid and wearing too many hats as it is.

Those are all excuses though. You matter. God has you in the role you are in for a reason. Just because others don't see the value of your role, doesn't take away from the reality that effective communications and marketing are vital for a church to reach people in today's world.

PR matters. It's what helps tell your story. It's not about covering up or spinning the truth. PR is about aligning the truth with the perception of the public so that you can clearly and effectively point people to Christ.

PR is everything, and your church doesn't get to dismiss it, because you're already doing it whether it's part of your job description or not.

JUSTIN DEAN

CHAPTER ONE

WHAT IS PR & WHY DOES IT MATTER?

"Everything you do or say is public relations."

- Someone smarter than me

Whether you like it or not we are all in public relations. You, the lead pastor, the coordinator, your admin, the community group leader, and all of your church members.

Someone, somewhere, once said, "Everything you do or say is public relations." I couldn't agree more. I would also add that in today's world, anything you *don't do* and *don't say* is also public relations.

When it comes down to it, what matters most about PR is actually not what you say, but rather what others say about you. Everything you do and don't do is perceived by someone else in a certain way. It doesn't matter so much what you meant, or how you feel, or what your intention was. The best marketing and advertising in the world doesn't matter if people don't understand the message.

What matters most is how people perceive it and how they feel about you because of it. What gets repeated and posted on social media, and told to their friends, is what they think you said - not necessarily what you actually said or meant.

Jean-Louis Gassee, a former Apple executive, defines it this way: "Advertising is saying you're good. PR is getting someone else to say you're good."

And another smart man, Stuart Ewen said, "The history of PR is… a history of a battle for what is reality and how people will see and understand what is reality."

The job of a public relations person is to manage perception in order to establish the best possible reputation for a person, company, or as we'll focus on in this book, a church. The reason we want to manage people's perceptions is so that we can align it with reality, and earn their trust. That trust leads to conversations about Jesus.

It is important for you to realize that you are already in public relations whether you want to be or not, and that your church needs to have an organized strategy in place to properly manage PR. Ideally this responsibility would fall on the plate of a Public Relations Manager or a Communications Director, but someone needs to own it.

The position and title can vary from church to church, but the important thing is that someone needs to be tasked with the responsibility of managing communications that affect the church's reputation and relationship with the public. Creating a positive perception of your church in the community provides a critical foundation for all other communication, so this is a very important role that shouldn't be overlooked or pawned off to a volunteer.

If you're reading this book, chances are you are this person. That's right, I just added one more thing onto your plate that I'm sure is already overflowing. Maybe you're an admin, or a coordinator, or maybe you're the Lead Pastor. The church world is much like a start-up - everyone's overworked, you're understaffed and under resourced. So adding PR to your already long list of duties might seem like an unnecessary burden. But remember, as I just said, you're already doing it. It's already on your plate. Now that you're aware of it, I can help you do it better.

The nice thing is, you don't have to shoulder all the weight by yourself. You or someone needs to lead the strategy, but the entire process needs to be a team effort.

Everyone in your church should be mindful of public relations, but leaving the decision making and strategy to a committee, or letting each manager handle his or her own communications, can lead to missed opportunities at the least, and a mismanaged crisis at the worst.

The opportunity is too great for this not to be the focus of someone in your organization. My friend Maggie Barragan, who currently heads up social media for Rock Church in San Diego, said at one of our conferences, "The church should be the good in the news."

When someone sees a positive story in secular news or on social media about your church, that's a huge victory and a massive opportunity to reach people who need to know Jesus. The church is the hope of the world, and we need to get better at shining light on that fact.

Pastor Greg Laurie, who leads Harvest Crusades and Harvest Christian Fellowship in Southern California, said in a recent sermon, "We live in a time of bad news, fake news, divisive news, and depressing news. As Christians, we need to recommit ourselves to getting the Good News out."

Are you actively promoting your church and the gospel

message to the public? Is your church actively pursuing opportunities to be in the news? Perhaps the thought of even responding to reporters makes you fearful and uneasy.

I understand that it's scary. But the more prepared you are, the easier it gets. Missing great opportunities to expose your church to new audiences is unfortunate, but the real scary part is not being prepared when your church is faced with a negative story.

Most people think of PR when a crisis hits. And frankly, by then it's too late. I often get calls from pastors and leaders at churches who are faced with their first crisis and don't know what to do. A pastor sleeps with someone he shouldn't sleep with, or someone is accused of something they say they didn't do, or protestors show up on a Sunday and no one has a plan. It could be as small as a negative comment on a social media post, but left unattended turns into a nightmare distraction.

While I love that my experience has led me to be able to help churches in need, I dread those calls. I don't mind helping - in fact, I love it. But more often than not, the church on the other end of the call isn't prepared and there's not much time to do anything about it.

There's only so much you can do at that point to minimize the damage and control the story.

And that's what PR is all about. Controlling the story. But not in the way you may be thinking. It's about keeping the narrative in the right lane. It's about building relationships and constantly having conversations that continue to tell our story and point people to what matters - Jesus.

We can't just do good and expect everyone to understand why, or even to notice. We have to tell them we did good, and why we did it. Through relationships and conversations, we can earn people's trust and respect so they'll talk about it and help spread our message.

Ultimately, we want people to understand who we truly are so that we open up more opportunities to tell them the truth about Jesus. But there will be times when others will be actively trying to show that you are something else. Whether it's reporters, or bloggers, or protestors, lawmakers and politicians, or people who have been hurt by the church, they'll try to eat away at your credibility and make it harder for you to stay on mission.

It takes someone who can actively craft the message to stay within the right context, amidst ever changing situations and attacks. That person also needs to be constantly building relationships, because only through real conversations and mutual respect between people do perceptions begin to change.

My friend Steven Dilla has found in all his research studying churches and people's behaviors, that people convert to community before they convert to Christ. Conversions and spiritual growth happen through relationships with each other. People come to church because they are invited. They stick around because they become known and start to feel like they belong. And they grow as disciples only once they believe.

We don't want to control the story so we can deceive and hide the truth from people. We want to control the story so we can make sure the truth stays in the light. Because it's the truth that will get them to trust us, become one of us, and ultimately lead them to Christ.

It can be a complex responsibility to own. There's a lot of room for abuse and mistakes. Namely, our own sinful desire to be liked and avoid conflict can tempt us to change the story or leave a part of the story out. Fear of man can tempt us to make mistakes we'll later regret. When we do make mistakes, the best thing we can do is own up to it, not try to hide it.

PR gets a bad rap because so many politicians and people in the business world have used it to try and hide their mistakes, or the mistakes of others. The PR team is called in to keep a story out of the news, by lying and applying manipulative techniques. Maybe they highlight a better story, or deflect the story onto competition. The worst part is that it works. That's why it's easy to abuse.

Churches haven't been perfect at PR either. Withholding truth and not answering questions can almost be as bad as covering something up or lying. Spinning facts in any way that makes people believe something that isn't quite the whole truth is just as sinful.

As Christians, we will still make mistakes but for us they are just another opportunity to model grace and repentance and show the world that we too are not perfect.

Be honest about your mistakes and use them to strengthen the narrative, not diminish it. We aren't perfect — that's why we need a savior. That's our story, and it's the greatest story ever told.

PR matters because without someone keeping the story straight, the world around us is going to keep knocking it off its track. If you don't tell your story, someone else will make one up for you. No one has an agenda to get your story straight, only you.

In fact, most people have their own agenda and they'll do anything to make your story fit into it. That not only damages your church and your reputation, it damages the reputation of all Christians and all churches, and makes it harder for everyone to point people to Jesus.

PR matters because every day it is getting harder and harder for anyone who wants to follow Jesus. Culture around us is becoming more and more hostile towards the gospel and biblical truths.

Not only that, but even among Christians we are seeing watered down versions of the gospel, all in the name of fitting in with the world so more people will like us and accept us. Biblical truths are being abandoned or manipulated in order to fill our buildings with more people. Many churches are adapting to the world around them instead of trying to lead it.

PR matters because too many churches are either drowning,

or staying out of the water, too afraid to even dip their toes in.

We must dive in and wade through the cultural chaos around us, preaching the gospel at all costs. It's not enough to just passively live a good life, do good works, and hope people come to Jesus. We must boldly speak the gospel, and do our best to handle persecution and backlash with as much grace and poise as possible.

The world's view of Christians is getting more and more distorted and perverted every day. It's time your church takes the steps to make public relations a priority so you can communicate the gospel in the most efficient and effective way.

CHAPTER TWO

THE MESS WE ARE IN

"We have created a world where the smartest way to survive is to be bland."

- Jon Ronson, Author of

So You've Been Publicly Shamed

We live in a world where there is no longer any expectation of privacy, and forgiveness is a thing of the past.

No longer can you make a joke between friends without risk of it being overheard and your photo and quote being tweeted out, wrecking your job and your family. No longer can honest mistakes be remedied with an apology between affected parties. No, you must be publicly shamed and your story forever entombed on the Internet. Even heartfelt repentance and apologies are scrutinized for their accuracy and truthfulness, and never accepted by the public as good enough restitution for your sins.

I was on a flight from Los Angeles to Atlanta recently and the guy next to me kept thrusting his back into his seat. It was obvious that the teenage girl behind him was kicking his seat or pressing too hard on the seat back screen. I looked back at the poor girl and saw she had a full cup of soda on the seat back tray.

By the third time the man thrust his seat back, I pulled out my earbuds and said, "Why don't you just ask her to stop? You're going to cause her to spill her drink."

The guy looked super annoyed and just ignored me. We live in a world where people are scared, or maybe too selfish, to have real conversations as human beings. We'd rather be passive aggressive jerks than actually confront someone and work out our differences.

I'm not even sure if the girl in the seat behind us was aware that she did anything to annoy the guy next to me. She probably thought he was just a jerk for thrusting his seat back so often, and didn't want to start a confrontation by asking him to stop.

I kept thinking about that guy on the plane and how had I not intervened, the situation may have escalated in a very bad way. In today's world, it was only a matter of minutes before the girl could have posted a photo of the guy to Twitter. Or the guy could have posted a photo of the girl drenched in soda with the hashtag #justice or #karma. Things like that happen all the time, and lives are ruined for no reason.

On that same flight, I had just finished Jon Ronson's book, *So You've Been Publicly Shamed*. In the book one of the many stories that Ronson shares is of a man who attended a conference for software developers. He was just an average Joe with a wife and kids. He and his buddy were sitting in a session at the tech conference and he made a nerdy but slightly inappropriate joke.

He said it to his buddy, not to a crowd, and not online. It wasn't even a good joke, or even a particularly crude joke. They're a bunch of nerds at a tech conference, what do you expect?

However, a young woman, apparently one of only a few women at the conference, was sitting in front of them. She turned around, snapped a photo of the two guys and proceeded to post the photo on Twitter calling them out for their "sexist jokes."

Her tweet went viral. The guy was shamed online by thousands of people and was fired from his job because of her post. All because she overheard his joke, took it out of context, and was offended. She could have turned around and told them she was offended, to which they most likely would have apologized and life would have gone on. Instead she turned immediately to public shaming on Twitter, and went a step further to include the photo. She didn't even talk to the guy.

It turns out the woman eventually got fired from her job too. Which she blames the guy for. To this day it doesn't look like she has taken any responsibility for her own actions, and continues to be somewhat of an activist fighting for the rights of female developers.

Sure, the guy should have been careful saying jokes out loud in a public place. But nobody deserves what he and his family had to go through. Do we really want to create a world where we can't tell any joke of any kind in a public place, for fear that someone might take it out of context and be offended—and then post our photo online for the world to publicly shame us?

I'm also reminded of the trouble that Clorox found themselves in with a controversial tweet posted April 8, 2015. The innocent tweet caused quite an uproar for a few days, and a ton of bad publicity for a brand that did nothing wrong.

Apple had just released a big software update for iOS that included a lot of new emoji icons, including more racially diverse faces. Before the update, you could only choose yellow faced emoji, but now you have the choice between many different skin colors including white, brown, and black.

Someone at Clorox wanted to capitalize on a big social

media news story and join the conversation by posting something they thought would be clever and creative, and it would have been if we didn't live in such an overly sensitive world.

People immediately took offense (shocking, I know!), and assumed that Clorox was implying the new black and brown skin tones should be bleached white.

Which is ludicrous considering that the emoji we had before the update were yellow, not white. And the graphic of the Clorox bottle that they posted didn't include any face emoji at all. I could understand if it was made up of nothing but black and brown faces, but it wasn't.

The problem was that the majority of the news stories and conversations about the iOS update were centered around the racial diversity of the new emoji, even though there were dozens of other new icons introduced, including my favorite, the taco emoji.

Clorox was focusing on the many household items that were included in the update, pointing out that a bleach bottle was not one of them.

The public conversation was focused on the new skin tones, so that's where people's minds went when they first read the tweet. Either Clorox was paying attention to the news stories and thought it wouldn't be an issue, so long as they were careful to not include face emoji's in the graphic they created, or they weren't paying close enough attention to the public conversation before trying to capitalize on it.

At the end of the day they could have used better judgement, but they didn't do anything wrong. I'm willing to bet it didn't even cross their minds that it would be an issue. Yet people immediately claimed they were racist and insensitive. "Ban Clorox" Facebook groups popped up. Hundreds of thousands of tweets were posted within hours.

It was clever and fun, and should have been a big marketing success. You would think that reasonable people would see the innocence of their tweet and move on. But people love a good fight, especially if a bunch of nobody's can take down a big brand. And especially if you can make race the center of the issue. You never know how the public is going to respond, nor can you predict what they'll get offended at next.

Clorox quickly deleted their tweet and posted another one, apologizing for the confusion:

"Wish we could bleach away our last tweet. Didn't mean to offend—it was meant to be about all the (toilet, bathtub, red wine) emojis that could use a clean-up."

They also put out a press release saying, "We apologize to the many people who thought our tweet about the new emojis was insensitive. It was never our intention to offend. We did not mean for this to be taken as a specific reference to the diversity emojis—but we should have been more aware of the news around this. The tweet was meant to be light-hearted but it fell flat."

An honest mistake. They apologized quickly. Life should move on. And it did eventually. Clorox isn't going anywhere, but this was a big hit. A smaller company would have buckled under this kind of pressure. I don't know if anyone got fired for this, but they certainly have in similar situations. I don't know what the financial impact of this mistake was, probably minimal in the long run. At the end of the day, this certainly was not the type of publicity that Clorox intended to get out of the tweet.

Stories like this are happening more often. Instead of us correcting this insane behavior, we put up with it, even promote it and encourage it. Half of the people reading this probably disagree with me, and still think Clorox was in the wrong. That's disappointing to me on so many levels. But the biggest disappointment from this, is that Clorox has yet to post anything that clever in the past two years. They went back to being bland.

Situations like this force all of us—people and brands— to become ultra private, sensitive and scared. It stifles creativity and boldness. We can neither be too liberal, nor too conservative. We must be perfect and flawless, never taking chances that could show us intolerant of anything. Not that anyone can keep up with what we are supposed to be tolerant of, or not, from week to week.

In Jon Ronson's book he says, "We have created a world where the smartest way to survive is to be bland."

This is how the world is these days. But it's worse for

Christians. We live in a world where a Christian bakery owner can't refuse to bake a wedding cake for a gay wedding, but a gay bakery owner can refuse to make a cake with scripture on it.

We live in a world where everything and anything is now tolerated, except being a bible-believing Christian. We are constantly being shamed, constantly losing our rights, and every day it is getting harder and harder to share biblical truths without severe repercussions. I can't think of any other religion or viewpoint that is more unaccepted in today's world. In a world where you can be whoever or whatever you want to be, being a Christian is becoming the exception.

The world wants Christians to be bland, but I say to hell with that. *See what I did there?*

When Christian media and bloggers start picking on churches and pastors, publishing unsubstantiated rumors and misinformation and participating in the shaming of someone who has made a mistake or sinned— even after they repent and apologize— then it's not the time to be bland, or tolerant. We can't let the world dictate what we do or say.

It's time to be bolder than we have ever been. It's time to stand up for the church, stand up for the Bible, and stand up for Jesus.

The church should be setting the culture, not adapting to it. Using the Bible and the Holy Spirit as our guide, we should be leading the way with what to believe and how to act. But too often we are trying too hard to stay relevant and not offend anyone.

I'm not saying we should get a pass to say and do what we want. Nor am I saying we shouldn't carefully craft our messages and pay attention to the conversation around us - because we should. I'm saying we need to stand up to a world that wants us to run away scared. We need to stand up for what's right.

This shouldn't be a shock. We knew this would happen. Being persecuted for being a Christian shouldn't surprise anyone who's read their Bible.

"...and you will be hated by all for my name's sake. But the one who endures to the end will be saved."

- Matthew 10:22

The truth is, they don't just want us to be bland. Being bland isn't enough. The world isn't going to stop there. If you think you can go about life being perfect, never making a joke in public, never making a mistake, and never saying anything ever that could be taken out of context— you're kidding yourself. It's not possible.

You can't wait for things to blow over, or for a better president to be elected. It will continue to get worse. That's a promise. If you think you can operate under the radar, and just play it safe, then shame on you. That's not what God has called us to do.

If you haven't read Mark Driscoll's book *A Call To Resurgence*, please pick it up. It was published amidst the closing of our church and didn't get the recognition it deserves. Had more church leaders actually read it, I'm convinced the church wouldn't be in as big of a mess.

In the book, Pastor Mark says, "With the epic rise of borrowed faith, lost faith, and no faith, what's left of actual Christian faith? The present-day blend of beliefs, traditions, and spiritualities makes it difficult to identify a remnant, especially when all of the ingredients have been marinated in the brine of American civil religion and Judeo-Christian ethics. Everything comes out of the mix with a hint of Christianity and vice versa."

He goes on, "Many Christians of the borrowed or lost faith variety have gladly accepted society's new vision for the church." *Since when does society dictate the church's vision?*

"In many of these congregations, the church favors *showing* the gospel and abandons *speaking* the gospel altogether. The problem is, the gospel cannot be shown; it must be spoken. Love, grace, mercy, justice, and the like can be shown with works. The gospel of Jesus Christ, however, must be spoken with words, because the gospel of Jesus Christ is not about our deeds but rather Jesus' deeds: his sinless life, substitutionary death, burial, and bodily resurrection for the salvation of sinners.[1]"

---

[1] A Call to Resurgence: Will Christianity Have a Funeral or a Future? by Mark Driscoll (Tyndale, 2013)

There's so much more. I could keep quoting, or you can pick up a copy of the book. The point is, the church has gone soft. Christian faith has lost any market share it had. It's hard to even tell who the real Christians are anymore.

In today's world it is increasingly difficult to share a clear gospel message, or even articulate what we believe.

We aren't safe. We never will be. Our only option is to continue sharing the gospel, spreading the Good News as far and wide as we can go, amidst whatever circumstances and scenarios that come our way.

Stay focused on telling the world about Jesus. Try new things to grow your church and reach more people. Take risks. Be Clorox. Operate within boundaries and be responsible (that's where a good PR plan comes into play), but don't be scared just because we live in a fallen world that doesn't understand us, and quite frankly is out to get us.

The most common problem facing the church right now is fear. Fear of losing people. Fear of negative comments on social media. Fear of protests over our beliefs. Fear that if we actually preach the gospel we'll lose our non-profit status, or lose our donors, or we'll be mocked and ridiculed. That fear has paralyzed the church.

But God tells us, "Fear not." In the Bible, it actually appears roughly 150 times. He doesn't tell us this because he knows it's going to get easier. It's not going to get easier. He tells us not to fear because he is with us. The Jesus who has experienced everything we're going through, and more, is with us and will never forsake us.

So wake up, church. It's time to get to work.

This is why having someone focused on communications can help. This is why PR matters. You need someone who can help set the boundaries. A good communications person is constantly analyzing trends in the world and how best to manage your message in a fickle tide of morals and political correctness. A good communications person would know what the conversation is about before entering it.

Mistakes will happen, and sin will enter the process. But that same communications person can help communicate repentance and restitution when necessary. The key is to take control of your message at all times. Again, not to spin it or manipulate it, but to make sure people are getting it right.

Your goal as a PR person is to make sure the gospel is actually being spoken, that your church stays true to it's vision and mission to save the world. And to ensure that the vision and mission doesn't get distorted into only doing good deeds so that you can better fit in to the world around you. Your good deeds shouldn't make you fit it, they should set you apart and point people to the gospel.

More important than promoting your latest food drive, or your attendance numbers at Easter, is showing the world that you too are a house full of sinners in need of grace. We need to show the world that we can take risks and be bold, and when we make mistakes we repent and make them right, but it doesn't change the story that we're trying to tell. Everything we do should point people to the gospel, otherwise what's the point?

Jesus didn't command us to go out into the world and be perfect. He certainly didn't call us to not offend anyone. He told us to worship him, and love one another. He told us to tell people about him - a man so controversial that we killed him, only for him to raise from the dead and free us of our sins.

It's your job to tell that story, and to tell that story well. Over and over again. No matter what.

Are you prepared?

CHAPTER THREE

TEN TRAITS OF A PR PERSON

"PR is a mix of journalism, psychology, and lawyering - it's an ever-changing and always interesting landscape."

- Ronn Torossian, 5W Public Relations

I will never forget my first official day on staff at a church. I had just left a great marketing position in the corporate world to now work for one of the largest and fastest growing churches in the world. When I signed up, I was excited to be using my skills and experience for such a great and worthy cause. I quickly realized I had no idea what I was getting myself into.

The position I had taken was the Public Relations Manager for the church, but the role evolved over the years, and I ultimately oversaw all public relations and communications for the church including content, social media, our websites, and more.

That first day was very revealing for me. As soon as I arrived at our cold, dank Seattle offices I was whisked off to meet with our senior pastor. He said something to me that helped set the tone for my role as the "Church PR Guy".

He asked if I was ready to strap my boots on. Which made me incredibly self-conscience about the Converse shoes I was wearing at the time. He went on to tell me that what I signed up for was not a job - but rather, it was a calling.

He said the office was full of people who worked nine to five and produced great content, but what we really needed were more soldiers on the frontline.

He told me I'd take a lot of hits. Not just for him, and not just for the church, but for God. That what we were trying to do was reach more people than ever with the story of the gospel, and that it was going to require risks, and would most definitely have its challenges. The only rewards we'd receive would be the satisfaction of seeing people's lives changed as they came to Christ and got baptized.

And we sure did reap the rewards. Year after year we saw hundreds of people get saved and over a thousand people per year get baptized. Hundreds of thousands of people watched our sermons and consumed our content every week, and we captured as many of their stories as we could.

It was incredible to be a part of it all, and I've yet to see anything else quite like it.

I walked away from that first meeting with a unbelievable weight on my shoulders that never went away. A glorious purpose that I had never felt before. I knew God had orchestrated everything in my life up until then so that I could serve in that role.

If you want to be successful in helping your church reach more people, you can't treat it like a job. If you feel called to this type of work, then the only thing left to do is strap your boots on and start to hustle. It's time to hone in on your skills and be the best you can be. People's lives are at stake.

When I was a little kid I never thought, when I grow up I want to be a public relations professional. Nobody says, "I want to work countless hours, promote other people's work, and only get the credit when something goes wrong."

I wanted to be a film director. Which has more to do with

the fact that I grew up in Los Angeles, and less to do with any talent I have in creating films or telling stories. I even took filmmaking classes, acting classes, and worked as an extra in a few movies (no, I won't be revealing which ones).

While I love movies and the whole filmmaking process, the problem was I'm actually not that creative. As it turns out, I'm better at promoting and marketing than I am at creating. But so are a lot of people - so what makes me unique?

What I came to find out over time, is that much like Liam Neeson's character in the movie *Taken*, I possess a unique set of skills that not a lot of people have.

No, I can't track down bad guys or kill people with my bare hands - although I've never tried. What I'm talking about are the skills and characteristics needed to be a successful communicator and public relations person for a church.

Not everyone can do this job well. In fact, you may currently be in this role at your church, and by the time you're done reading this book you may realize this isn't your calling.

If that happens, I hope you'll trust in God to help you find a place to serve that brings you satisfaction and brings him the most glory.

I also hope that I'll be able to give you enough practical advice and tools to help you do your job even better, whether you continue to take on this burden or you share the responsibility with a team.

If you can nail down these following skills and traits, or assemble a team that can, then you're ready to start building a solid PR plan for your church.

Your desire to see people come to Jesus, and your willingness to work hard at spreading his message is what matters most. When it comes down to it, the following skills can be learned or outsourced, but they're important nonetheless. I'm a firm believer in training the called, rather than calling the trained.

In my experience, I believe a good church PR person should have the following ten traits and characteristics to be successful:

1. Good Discernment
2. Trustworthy
3. Thick Skinned
4. Adventurous
5. Humble

6. Critical Thinker
7. Good Writer
8. Sociable
9. Informed
10. Dedicated

GOOD DISCERNMENT

This may be the most important characteristic of a good PR person, especially in the church setting. Without good discernment, you'll likely make a lot of mistakes and miss a lot of opportunities, so think long and hard in this area and get the assistance of people who know you to shed some light on whether this is a quality you possess.

I believe discernment is a spiritual gift[2]. Pray and ask God to give you the gift of discernment if that is your desire.

Good discernment is more than just knowing the difference between right and wrong. Discernment involves being in tune with the Holy Spirit and being able to act swiftly on his guidance. It's more than just good judgement. In fact, I would say discernment is what kicks in when you aren't sure about something but still need to make a decision.

It's the feeling in your gut about something when you don't have all the information. It's also that feeling in your gut when the information tells you one thing, but you're sure it's wrong anyway.

When I look back on the mistakes I've made as a PR person, most of them were when I acted or said something that went against my gut. When I went by the book even though I felt it inside me that I should do or say something else.

As a PR person, you need to be able to think quick on your feet. Things move fast, deadlines come and go, news cycles can be as short as a few hours, and often opportunities are thrown in your face with little time to research.

At our church, we would get strange requests almost every week, either through email or the main phone number, and sometimes when someone stops by.

As the head of PR, I would be notified about all of these

---

[2] See I Corinthians 12:10, Hebrews 5:14, Acts 5:3-6;16:16-18 and 1 John 4:1

requests, often having to make the decision on how we responded.

Sometimes it was a church member who thought that we should take a stronger and more public stance on homosexuality and gay marriage. Other times it would be someone who believed God spoke to them and had a message for our senior pastor. And a lot of times it was simply someone who just wanted to debate theology, or rebuke us for something that we said or didn't say.

We took every request seriously, although it was often easy to filter through requests that were so crazy or so negative that there wasn't anything we could do. Most of those got a canned pre-written response and we went on our way.

However, some requests were legit. Either someone was hurting and needed pastoral care or some other assistance from the church. Or sometimes we did say or do something wrong, and needed to make it right. And other times people were alerting us to very real concerns about the church or a specific individual.

Navigating through these requests and choosing what got our time and resources, and what didn't, required a lot of discernment. These were real requests from real people, and my decisions affected real lives.

One day a request came in over the phone to our receptionist. On any other day, this request would have easily went into our queue and eventually would have received a standard response. But something tugged on my gut that day and I knew this one deserved my attention.

A man called in and told our receptionist that he needed to speak with someone in senior leadership. He refused to give any details, just that it was serious and not just any pastor would do.

The receptionist wasn't about to patch him through to our senior pastor. That just wasn't something we would do. The guy was relentless and wouldn't let her just take a message. He knew he would be brushed off. To be fair, we've had other calls like this that ended up just being someone who wanted to tell our pastor off, and it's hard as a receptionist to tell who is being reasonable and who is a crazy person.

I was alerted about the call, as was normal procedure when something weird or tense was happening. Like I said, any other day and I'd tell this guy to cool down and submit his request in writing. But something was off. My spidey-senses were tingling, and I knew I should take this seriously.

I told the guy that there's no way he was going to talk to our pastor, but that I would listen to him and take whatever action was appropriate. That was the only option I gave him, so he gave in. But he didn't want to do it over the phone, and he didn't want to put anything in writing.

I agreed to meet him. I had no idea what I would be walking into, so I told him to meet me at a Starbucks that was next door to one of our church campuses. I took a friend and fellow church staffer with me for accountability… and for protection (he's a big guy with tattoos).

As it turns out, the guy wasn't a church goer. He wasn't even a Christian. But he had information that I am glad he brought to us. A friend of his had a teenage daughter, whom one of our lay pastors had been messaging privately with on Facebook.

The guy showed me print outs of their conversations, which he obtained through the teenage girl's mother. As I read the transcripts, the pastor, who was a volunteer and also worked at a local high school, was clearly flirting with this underage girl. And to make it worse, I knew he had a wife and children of his own.

I assured the man that we would handle the situation and not ignore it, and thanked him for bringing it to our attention. I asked for his phone number so that I could follow up with him should I have any questions, and so that I can give him an update on what we had done about it.

I immediately called our Executive Pastors and alerted them about the situation, and they agreed that my next move should be to alert the school where the pastor worked, as well as the police. While I made those phone calls, they visited the lay pastor's wife.

The pastor admitted to his wrongdoing, and was immediately removed as a pastor and fired from his job at the school. The weight of turning this man's life upside down was upon me, but all I could think about is that poor teenage girl who probably didn't know what she was getting into. Based on the conversations I read, it would have escalated into something far worse had this friend not intervened.

We continued to provide pastoral care to the pastor and his family, and we offered to pay for counseling and legal aid for the teenage girl and her family. The pastor did eventually face criminal charges and I pray that he and his family have been restored.

I was prepared with statements for the press should anything be leaked, but the whole mess stayed out of the news thanks to our fast reactions as well as the grace of the man who brought it to our attention. This wasn't particularly something we wanted to release on our own, but we were prepared to share every detail should it come up.

Had I not trusted my gut that day, the man was prepared to release those transcripts to the news and the police. We would have lost any leverage to tell the story correctly, and would have been forced to be on the defensive. The man didn't expect us to do the right thing, but we did. When I called him to give him an update on everything that had been done, he thanked me and said we turned around his perception of the church.

TRUSTWORTHY

A good PR person needs to be discreet and trustworthy. We often deal with sensitive information, such like the story I shared above. At the time, there was no reason for the information around that story to be released to anyone else. As a PR person, you have to be able to keep a lot of things to yourself.

As much as I love to share about myself on social media, when it came to my work I rarely shared anything. There's a time and place for sharing certain information, while other information needs to be kept more private. You have to be able to know the difference and always act in the best interest of the church and of those involved.

Sometimes this means you know something about people that others don't, and you can't ever share about it. You can't even hint about it. I would sometimes be looped in on things that were so sensitive or private, that I would be told, "Don't even share this with your wife." We didn't want to put the pressure on her to have to remember what was sensitive and what wasn't.

I'm not talking about hiding anything - this would be stuff like a church discipline case that was confidential, or a private situation with a pastor that was still being resolved. Sometimes it was hard being involved in serious situations and not being able to go home and talk about them with my wife.

As communicators who are often tasked with blasting out message after message promoting this and that, it can also be hard to balance that with information you need to keep sensitive.

Sometimes it's not even that it's sensitive, it's just that

releasing it at a later time will have a greater effect, so you must be patient.

Pastors need to also understand that your PR person is your public defender. Don't withhold information from them. The communications person should have a holistic and inclusive picture of everything going on and be able to speak into it. You don't want them caught off guard, because that can be damaging to your overall message.

Give them a seat at the table and authority to tell you the truth. If you can't trust your PR person to know everything, then there's either an issue with them or with you. Either way you need to figure it out and make a change.

THICK SKINNED

PR isn't always going to be easy. If it is, then you're doing something wrong. You're going to need thick skin if you want to make it past your first crisis or even your first encounter with the press.

Part of my job was reading and reviewing everything that was said about the church online. Anytime someone would make a comment on an article, post a blog post, tweet, or even sneeze within a mile of our church - I would know about it. We had alerts and monitoring services running 24/7 so I'd know the second something breaks.

That's probably overkill for the majority of churches, but at the time we would get a ton of media attention online. I monitored what people said, because we cared what they said. People having a perception of us that aligned with reality was critical to us being able to reach even more people all over the world with the story of Jesus Christ.

Sometimes what they would say was pretty harsh. We were the largest church in the Seattle area, an overly liberal and pretty hostile setting for a conservative, reformed Christian church.

As the official spokesperson for the church, often their criticisms and nasty comments were directed at me personally. That was more of an issue for my wife than it was for me. No wife likes reading bad things about their husbands in the local paper, or worse on national stages like Slate or the New York Times.

I ordered a pizza once and the delivery driver texted me to say that he knew who I was and where I worked, so he wouldn't be delivering me my pizza. That's what I mean by hostile. The guy had recognized my name from news stories about the church, and decided it was worth risking his job to tell me that he wasn't going to deliver my pizza to me. That was a scary time. This guy I had never met hated me that much, and now had my address. We were thankful for security during that time.

You probably think you won't ever experience anything quite that extreme in your position, but I would have said the same thing before it happened to me.

I learned to let things like that roll off my shoulders. Sure, it hurts, and boy did I want to fight back and defend myself. But you have to put the church first. You have to have the willpower to not flame the fires. You have to stay on message and stay on mission. Sometimes it can be quite a sacrifice.

ADVENTUROUS

If playing it safe is your thing, then you're going to be a lousy PR person. I don't care if your church is a 150-year-old Baptist Church in Alabama, if you want to reach more people and get some attention then you're going to need to be bold and adventurous. (No offense to Alabama Baptists, I'm sure you're a lot of fun.)

Being bold and adventurous doesn't mean foolish and arrogant. But you need to be able to push the envelope and be a little different. As churches, we are fighting against a lot of preconceived notions, and we're trying to reach a world that doesn't want us to reach them. Untuck your shirt, roll up your sleeves, and break out of the box.

Paul says, "For to me to live is Christ, and to die is gain.[3]" That means, don't be afraid to die, but it also means don't be afraid to live. We are here for a purpose. Let's make it count.

Clorox was adventurous with their emoji tweet a few years back. It may not have turned out how they wanted, but that beats sitting around being a boring old bleach company.

---

[3] Philippians 1:21 "For to me to live is Christ, and to die is gain." (ESV)

Wendy's is also adventurous. Amy Brown is currently the woman who manages social media for the fast food restaurant chain. Her and her team are known for their sass on the official @wendys Twitter account. It's how they amassed over a million followers and growing, as well as national acclaim. What's impressive is that it's more than just shock and awe. They provide helpful customer service through their Twitter account, including rewarding people for their loyalty. Almost every person who interacts with them gets a reply, which makes people feel loved and appreciated.

Their funny, cavalier attitude has helped establish brand loyalty with many customers, myself included, and continues to keep them in the conversation. No one talks about how cool McDonald's is, they all talk about how funny Wendy's is. Go check out their account, it's not what you'd expect from a typical fast food place, and the church can learn a ton from them.

HUMBLE

Sometimes you've got to take a backseat. As a PR person, you're usually promoting someone else to the spotlight, and you need to be ok with that.

We're the people behind the curtain, mouthing the words to the speech being shared on stage because we're the ones who wrote it. You need to be ok with your work being attributed to someone else's name, and not getting the recognition for it.

Sure, sometimes you get quoted in a big newspaper or you get to go on TV to talk about something cool, but even then it's not about you - it's about what you are promoting.

Our job is to make the gospel the hero, and get out of the way. If the story becomes about you and what you said, then you did something wrong.

CRITICAL THINKER

You need to be able to see the negative angle in things, so you can plan ahead and react when necessary. While at the same time not being a jerk about it or letting it get to you.

Nobody likes the person who constantly points out what is wrong, but there's still a responsibility to know so you can learn from it. While others are still celebrating the wins, you're already thinking one step ahead or making notes on what could have been done better for next time.

Practically this means digging deeper into that "great blog post" that someone just wrote, and making some assumptions about how it will be perceived by different audiences. What might seem innocent to some, could be offensive to others. It's your job to determine if it's a big enough deal to change, or if you're going to roll with it. If you roll with it, you've got to make a plan to defend it.

It means being the person who says, "That's a great tweet,

and I love how bold we are being, but can we post it next week so we don't distract from Easter?"

This also means you often have to think like the bad guys. Put yourself in the mindset of the blogger who always criticizes your church. Try to think like the reporter who always writes negative stories about you. What can you change to avoid another publicity nightmare? It can be emotionally and physically draining, but someone has to do it.

GOOD WRITER

You don't have to be a great writer, but you should be a good one. You have to be able to articulate yourself well in writing. From speeches, to statements, to tag lines, to ad copy, to blog posts, to headlines, to sound bites… you're going to be tasked with crafting those messages and you better be good at it.

At the very least, you better have the resources to hire a good writer who's on hand to help you. I never thought of myself as a great writer. That's why I usually get someone to help me. You'll be at an advantage if writing isn't a struggle for you.

I'll write something I love, then I'll read something a good writer has written and immediately see my inadequacies. I was fortunate enough to have a team of writers working for me at our church. We produced so much content each week that it was definitely needed. Between the two major blogs that my team managed, we were producing about 15 to 20 posts per week on top of ebooks and other assignments. Luckily with several writers, editors, and theologians on staff, I could send over a poorly written blurb and get back a theologically and grammatically sound essay in return.

SOCIABLE

One of the key roles of a PR person, particularly at a church, is to build relationships. Your whole goal is to align the public's perception with the message of your church, so that requires actually interacting with the public from time to time.

It helps if you're sociable. You have to genuinely like people and want to be around them, or at least be really good at faking it.

Relationships are the key to everything you are going to do as a church communicator. We'll dig deeper into this later, but the idea is to form and maintain healthy and candid relationships with the media, bloggers, people in the community, business owners, influencers, celebrities, and more. The more people who know you, the easier you can get your true message out.

While most church communicators seem to be introverts who like to hide behind their iPhone screen, you might want to make sure someone on your team is good at talking with people and making friends. This is going to be a major part of what you do if you want to successfully manage the perception of your church.

INFORMED

A good PR person is someone who is always informed. I've talked about having a pulse on the perception of the church and monitoring what people are saying about it - that's just one part.

A successful PR person is up to date on trends in the media, trends with social networks, trends in culture, what other churches are doing, what successful businesses and brands are doing, breaking news, the political climate, new laws, and more. The more knowledge you can consume and soak in, the better you will understand the world around you and the context in which you are doing ministry. The better you understand that, the better you can prepare your church to help communicate the gospel to the world.

Additionally, you need to have open communication with your church leaders. Your communications department, whether it's just you or a larger team, can't be alone on an island and only activated when there's a crisis or something big to communicate. You need to be read in on how the church is doing, where it's going, how its struggling and how it's succeeding. You should have a good grasp on the bigger picture - the whole picture - so you can ensure the things your church is saying and doing are aligning with the direction you want to go and the perception that you want to have.

There's nothing idle about this critical role in the church.

It's a noble calling to be the communications person. And I may be the only person to ever acknowledge that for you.

Aside from your pastor and the preaching of your church, this is the most critical piece of the mission - defending, promoting and distributing that message as far and wide as it can go, in the best possible way. It's a tough task and requires you to constantly be on your feet and ready for action.

DEDICATED

This is a tiring and thankless job at times. And it doesn't stop. You're on call 24/7 every day of the year. The news doesn't even stop for Christmas - in fact that's a great time to get some wonderful stories out about what your church is doing in your community.

You've got to be dedicated to sustain it. It's a lifestyle that you have to get used to. My hope is that you won't take a job like this halfheartedly. My goal is to encourage churches to take risks and grow like they've never grown before. That's going to take dedication from people like you in the trenches and on the front lines.

Hear this though, there's no shame in serving in a PR role for a season, then taking a break. It's a tough job, and even though many people won't see it that way, it's not worth destroying your health or family over. So stay dedicated, but know your limits and take advantage of your down time.

While there certainly are other traits and characteristics that make a good PR person, I believe these are the most important. If you can be all of these, or most of these, then you'll last a very long time in your role and hopefully make a huge impact for your church.

If you need to improve in one or two of these areas, start focusing on them now. Start by praying and asking God, should he want you to continue doing what you are doing, that he would help you develop in those areas. Then reach out to others, your pastor, your boss, your colleagues, and ask them to keep you accountable in those areas.

If you're taking on multiple roles in your church, and you simply can't be all of these qualities, try hiring consultants or volunteers who excel in the areas where you need help.

If you're not a good writer, hire a writer. If you have someone eager to get out in the community and build relationships, equip them to go do it well. If you're more comfortable behind the scenes, but you know someone eager to get on camera, let them be your figurehead and you craft what they say.

Not everyone is built to be all of these things, but if you work as a team and admit your shortcomings, you can make it work.

CHAPTER FOUR

CREATING A PR PLAN

"Public relations are a key component of any operation in this day of instant communications and rightly inquisitive citizens." **- Alvin Adams, American Businessman**

By the time you are done with this book, you will have everything you need to create a PR plan for your church.

A PR plan is vital for your church to survive in today's world. It shouldn't be an afterthought, or a low priority. If in fact your mission is to reach more people and point them to Jesus, then a PR plan is going to outline your strategy to carry out that mission and what to do if things go wrong. Simply put, do ministry without one and you'll be less effective, and more vulnerable.

Again, it's imperative that you realize you are already in the PR game, whether you choose to be or not. You can either play the game with no plan at all, and hope that you'll not only survive, but that you'll do well, or you can plan ahead and try to be the best you can be. By God's grace, most churches alive today are carrying on with nothing more than hope and grace as a plan. Only time will tell how long that plan will last for them.

Hope and grace should be a part of every plan, but by itself that's not much of a plan at all. God knew we would be doing ministry in the world that we currently live in. He knew the context and climate of the community he's placed you and your church in. He knew we'd have enormous opportunity with the internet, social media, television, newspapers, blogs, apps, smartphones, and more.

In Jesus' day, people used the tools they had at the time to spread the gospel to the communities they visited. We need to use the tools of our time to spread the gospel to all the nations. A written PR plan will help you stay organized and on mission as you carry out your goals.

Your PR plan should include the following sections:

- PR Goals and Objectives
- Communications Guide
- Media Relations Plan
- Social Media Strategy and Policies
- Content Strategy
- Crisis Plan

Your plan can include more than this, but these are the core sections you should have. We will cover each of these in depth, and I provide a lot of the groundwork for you, so don't panic just yet.

Keep in mind that this isn't a marketing or advertising plan. This should precede and help support any marketing plans you have to promote and advertise your church or certain programs.

The objective of a PR plan is to document how you plan to help manage the perception of the church with the public, so that it aligns with your overall mission, vision, and goals. It should also prepare your church for action should something go wrong.

SET YOUR PR GOALS

A documented plan will also help you measure your

progress and performance. Without a written plan in place, that names your goals and objectives, you'll have a hard time distinguishing what is working and what is not working.

It is often said that public relations cannot be effectively measured, and therefore cannot be properly planned and budgeted for. That may be true if your plan is just to sit idly by and react to whatever happens. But a pro-active plan can be measured a number of different ways, especially in today's modern world of technology and data.

Start your PR plan by stating your goals, even if they must be in broad terms. That way you know what to measure against. I suggest dividing your PR goals into three different types:

REPUTATION MANAGEMENT GOALS

These are goals that deal with the perception of the church and its leaders in the community or online. An example would be: "We plan to improve positive opinions and mentions of our church in the public," or "We want to improve our search results so positive stories about the church show up on Google searches."

If possible, get more specific, such as with whom you plan to focus your attention, and by what date, etc. Otherwise it's fine to keep these goals generic.

RELATIONSHIP MANAGEMENT GOALS

Relationship goals focus on how the church connects with the media and others in the community. We'll learn more about the different types of relationships in the next chapter.

An example could be: "We plan to improve communication with the public, local and national media, and others in the community."

To get more specific you can state which media publications you want to develop relationships with, or which organizations and businesses in the community you plan to reach out to.

TASK MANAGEMENT GOALS

This is where you'll specifically lay out the PR tasks you wish to achieve. For example: "Our goal is to increase attendance at our member's meetings by 30%," or "We plan on pitching four new press releases to media contacts per month."

Setting these goals will not only help you better manage your PR efforts, but it can also help your leaders better manage the resources and budget that can be allocated towards reaching these goals. The more detailed you are with the reason why you need to focus on PR, the more specific you can be with your budgeting and staffing asks.

Get more specific by including measurable items like dates, resources, and staffing costs. What software and apps do you need to achieve these goals, and what do they cost? How many hours per week will it take your communications coordinator to write and pitch press releases? How many hours will it take per week to schedule social media posts and engage with followers?

It is also critical for the success of your efforts, and the success of your church, that the goals you lay out in your PR plan line up with and support the overall goals of the church in general. How do your PR goals help achieve your church's mission?

Your PR plan should reinforce your mission, not compete with it or run parallel to it. Any story you help support through interviews, press releases, blog posts, social media posts, etc. should help tell the story of how Jesus is carrying out this mission through your church.

COMMUNICATIONS GUIDE

A communications guide is the section of your PR plan that helps distinguish the processes and guidelines needed to effectively communicate through each of your channels.

It should include your communications best practices such as a writing and style guide, branding guidelines, official bios of key leaders, and your official answers to frequently asked questions. It should be the definitive guide on how and why you talk about certain things, and which things to avoid.

Think through the things that you communicate often, and include guidelines for them in your communications guide. The idea is to minimize the amount of duplicate work you and your teams have to do, as well as to ensure your communications are always consistent and inclusive.

For example, if you often plant new churches, then you may want to include information on how you talk about new church plants as well as what typically goes into a plan for each church. If you hold a big event every year such as a carnival or a certain sermon series, include al the pertinent information needed to communicate well.

Your writing and style guides should include things like the proper way to address pastors and deacons in your church, as well as the proper way to use your church name in writing. How and where should your logo be used? What are the official fonts and colors to be used in documents and graphics?

It should also speak to the tone and type of voice you want your church to have. Is it friendly, or professional?

COMMUNICATIONS CHANNELS

Your Communications Guide should also include a list all of your available marketing and communications channels and resources. This will likely be something you update frequently as your organization grows and programs are added and taken away.

Communications channels are any medium where you can interact with an audience, whether passively or actively. Your social media platforms such as Facebook and Twitter are both communications channels. Email, your printed bulletin, billboards, Facebook ads, stage announcements, slides on screens, t-shirts, your website, your app, etc. The list will be rather lengthy when you actually start documenting it all.

Once you have a list of your channels you'll know what you have to deal with. You'll also be able to see where you may be missing something, as well as areas that you can eliminate because they are redundant, or not kept up with. For example, most churches who go through this process for the first time don't realize how many individual Facebook pages the church has until they list them all out. If a Facebook page isn't being properly updated and utilized, or it can be just as effective to use one of the other pages, then you may want to disable some of them.

This list of communications channels will come in handy as you're creating marketing and advertising plans. Consult with it every time you have something to promote, whether it be a sermon series, an event, or a ministry. Ask yourself, *what are the best channels to communicate this particular program or event?*

Which channels you choose will also depend on what else is being promoted at the same time. Just because you're using your Facebook page to promote Event A, doesn't mean it makes sense to also promote Event B there right now. A communications calendar, even if it's a simple spreadsheet, that shows everything going out on each channel can be an incredible effective tool for this.

Listed next to each communications channel should also be the name of who owns that channel. Who is the gatekeeper before something is released on your Facebook page, or before an email is sent to your entire list? Who gets to pitch stories to the media or reply to requests from reporters? Who ultimately decides what gets announced from stage? Who has to tell the youth pastor no when there are already too many announcement slides being displayed before service?

Documenting your channels, the keepers of each channel, and even the processes needed to use each channel, can help your church get more organized and keep everyone on the same page. It can also help minimize confusion and clarify your message. Too many messages going out on a single channel can result in none of the messages being heard.

CREATE AN FAQ

I highly recommend that you develop a list of Frequently Asked Questions and your official answers to include in your plan.

Think through common questions that your church gets asked a lot, or questions that you know will come up if your church receives more publicity.

Prepare responses to those questions ahead of time so you aren't having to do so on the fly. Put those questions and your responses into your PR plan and distribute them to your key staff. This way everyone is on the same page and has the same answer when something comes up.

These could be questions about your core beliefs, or the way you operate church. It should include controversial items, such as your stance on homosexuality, women in pastoral roles, church discipline procedures, church membership, etc. I would also include church history items, such as how and when the church began, how you describe key milestones, and how you describe the vision for the future.

I think it's wise to add this FAQ to your website, so it's open and transparent, and so there's an official place to point people to for answers.

...

We'll cover media relations, social media, content, and crisis planning in the coming chapters, but before we go one I want to make sure you first understand the importance of relationships.

CHAPTER FIVE

RELATIONSHIPS MATTER

"Relationships are leverage. If you give value to someone else first, you have leverage. It's as simple as that."

- Gary Vaynerchuk,

Author and CEO VaynerMedia

The most important part of public relations is relationship building. Relationships are what set public relations apart from marketing and advertising.

Marketing is the overall process of boosting awareness of something to a specific audience. It is focused on promoting and selling a specific product or service. Traditionally this is done through paid TV, radio, and print advertisements, as well as through ads and messages on social media and digital platforms. Think of it as telling a person how they should feel or what they should do.

Whereas, public relations is all about managing the perception and reputation of the brand as a whole. It's about managing how people feel and react to whatever it is you are promoting through your marketing and advertising efforts.

Practically it means leveraging relationships to get people to talk about you and what you have to offer. It has been said that "advertising is paid media, public relations is earned media." When a third party shares their perspective or feelings about your product, service, or company then that's public relations at work.

Through relationship building we can get people to start talking about your church and ensure that the overall public perception aligns with who you really are and what you care about.

So, who should you be building relationships with? I believe you should be building and maintaining relationships with everyone and anyone. The more people who know about your church and develop a positive perception of your church, the better.

However, there are a few categories of people that should strategically be a part of your public relations plan:

- Press and Media (local and national media contacts)
- Bloggers
- Other Churches
- Your Community (online and offline)
- Thought Leaders

The key to maintaining great relationships with these groups is to get to know them and anticipate their needs. Then provide them as much value as you can.

Let's look at each type of relationship you need to build, and how we can better get to know them and their needs.

PRESS & MEDIA

Whether it comes to pitching a story or replying to an inquiry from a reporter, relationships are going to be what matters most.

You can send out a pitch every week and never see your church in the news. Everyone knows controversy, sex, and scandal are what sells. So why would a reporter write about your food drive, or how great your Easter services are going to be?

This is where building relationships with reporters, journalists, editors, and bloggers can really come in handy. If they know you and respect you already, then your pitches are going to be taken more seriously. In fact, if done right, they won't even seem like pitches.

Getting to know your reporters is key in being able to help them get the story right. Often times you're going to be putting the responsibility of sharing the story of your church — and hopefully the gospel — with someone who is not a believer. The chances of them articulating it well enough to the public are slim. It depends on how well you communicated it to them, but it also has a lot to do with how well they know you and trust you.

When it comes time to promote something good that your church did, you're going to need the press to spread the word. Your blog and your Twitter account only reach a select audience of people who are already your fans. An article in a local newspaper, or a spot on the evening news can help you reach a wider audience of unchurched people.

Or when a false accusation is thrown your way, it's going to be a lot easier to get your quote out there when you have somebody you already know to work with. You can't just send out press releases and hope they pick up on the story or get your side of it right.

Getting to know your local reporters is easier than you think. Start by making a media contact list for your area.

BUILDING A MEDIA CONTACT LIST

Using an app like Feedly, subscribe to RSS feeds from all the major papers, as well as the smaller ones, even the community papers and blogs. As you read and skim through the articles about your community, take note of who is writing articles that you enjoy. Pay particular attention to anyone writing articles about your church, and other churches in the area.

Then email everyone on that contact list and send them a personal greeting. If you liked something in an article they wrote, link to the article and tell them what you liked. Use this as a way to introduce yourself to them. Don't ever pitch them a story on your first contact. Just introduce yourself, offer some flattery, and leave them with your contact information. You're just flirting a bit, not asking them to marry you just yet.

Here's an example of what you can send to a local reporter that you want to get to know:

Hi, my name is Justin and I'm the Communications Director at Local Church. I noticed you write a lot about the local community here in the neighborhood and I wanted you to know we appreciate your work. The article yesterday about the food bank was powerful. Thanks for taking the time to share so many details about the families they are serving. That kind of stuff is super important to us. If you ever need anything or want to chat about our church just let me know. I wanted to make sure you had a contact person here, so please find my personal cell number below.

I didn't ask or expect anything. It was casual and loose. I was just saying hello, complimenting them, and making sure they had my contact info. Now if something about the church comes up, they have a name and direct phone number of someone to call. And in my experience, they will. I sent out an email like that to a local reporter and the next article they wrote included a quote from me and was a more complete story.

Had I not reached out to them they would have either published without our input, or they would have had to go through all the trouble of trying to find someone to talk to at our church.

Put yourself in their shoes and get to know their needs. Reporters usually have multiple articles they have to get out per day. The less time they have to spend hunting people down for quotes, the better. So they're going to call who they know first.

This means when they're fishing for an extra story, you want to be accessible to them. It was one thing to get a call when they were following up on a story about us. But once I started building relationships with these reporters, I started getting cold calls from them fishing for stories when it was slow. Those were the best, because that gave us an opportunity to be on the offense and not the defense. We could share about the great things we were doing and get more exposure for the church. Articles that typically wouldn't see the light of day were actually getting published.

That is an important goal of building relationships with reporters and journalists — to be able to earn their trust and respect by providing value, so you can gain better opportunities to share what is going on at your church. When that happens, we get to be in a position of influence over the community and culture around us.

I had an interesting encounter with a well-known Christian news website early on in my ministry role. There was a certain reporter who was constantly writing what I would call hit pieces on the church. Most of the time her articles were full of misinformation and exaggerations. In articles that were clearly news stories and not opinion pieces, she would let her bias against our church shine brightly.

Despite my efforts to contact her and offer our side of the story, she never once interviewed me or contacted us despite writing about us almost weekly.

I finally reached out to her editor and simply told him that we expected more from a Christian news organization. We really believed at the time that they were positioned to be the leading voice in the media for the church as a whole, and it was disappointing that they were letting such nonsense about us be published on their site, presumably just to get more page views.

I also let him know what I did like. There was another reporter at the time who also wrote about our church pretty frequently. His articles weren't always in our favor, but they were always balanced and well thought out, and he always had the decency to reach out to me for quotes and more information. He is part of a dying breed of journalists who actually respect their craft and respect other people, and working for a Christian news organization it was clear he loved the church.

I simply explained to the editor the difference between this reporter and the one who kept slamming us, and how we'd be more than willing to work with them so long as they acted like real journalists. To their credit, the editor quickly took action to make things right. Within a few days we were notified that the reporter was let go from staff and her articles were removed from the site. Apparently, some of them had been published without an editor even reviewing them first. This is how it works in today's world of ad revenue and page views. Aa a smaller online only media outlet, they were just trying to keep up and stay alive, but at the expense of our reputation.

I was shocked to hear this. I told the editor that if they didn't even have control over their own newsroom then we were going to shut them out completely. I wasn't asking for the articles to be more positive about us, I just wanted them to at least have the decency to reach out to us and to follow proper editorial standards. If the articles weren't positive anyway, I had nothing to lose by being a bit aggressive with them.

I told him I had hoped to give them unfettered access to me and the church if they ever needed quotes or clarification on a story, but not if they continue to let their reporters go unchecked. I knew we had a bit of leverage, because articles with our church and pastor featured in them obviously did well on their site, or they wouldn't keep writing them.

A few days later the editor called me back and wanted to let me know about additional changes they were making in the organization based on my feedback. They completely revamped their editorial process, and assured me that they were taking steps to become a more reputable news organization. He even invited me to attend their weekly conference calls with the editorial management team so I could listen in on the changes being made and the way they were pitching stories. It was thrilling to be a part of that process for a few months.

I continued to build on the relationship with the other reporters and the editor, and it resulted in pretty consistent coverage on what the church was doing. We were also able to submit a ton of op-ed pieces and articles of our own. Even when they'd write articles that weren't so positive, they'd add our voice and our side to the story. And when we had something to share, they were more receptive to publishing something about it.

It paid off to stand up to them and offer them candid feedback on how we were being treated. I knew a better way was possible, and wasn't afraid to ask for it. It set the tone for how I handled my relationships with most reporters, even at large secular news organizations. It didn't always work out, but it helped me know who to filter out and who to continue developing relationships with.

You're not going to be friends with everyone. The local "alternative" newspaper in Seattle, for example, was never fair in their coverage of us. They are an ultra-liberal, very anti-Christian organization, so it wasn't surprising. It got to the point with them where it wasn't worth even replying to their inquiries because we always ended up being misquoted and entirely misrepresented.

Knowing your local reporters well can also have a lasting impact on the kingdom that you may not have even considered. We got a call one day at our church from the Seattle Times. They were planning on doing a big feature story on the church and wanted to send a photo-journalist to shadow the senior pastor for a day.

They sent an award-winning photographer and journalist to capture the story as the lead pastor of one of the fastest growing churches in America.

After a day of following our pastor around, riding in his truck, and learning about his life, the reporter gave his life to the Lord. He later left his bustling news career and went on to become a pastor, leading our largest church campus.

You never know how God is going to use a story about your church. We encountered plenty of other stories where someone read an article about us, even not so positive ones, and decided to give our church a try for themselves. I guess that's why they say no press is bad press.

BLOGGERS

In his book *Trust Me, I'm Lying*, self-proclaimed media manipulator Ryan Holiday explains how he was successful in marketing movies, books, and other products for his clients by exploiting stories through small niche blogs and trading his stories up the chain to larger sites, news organizations and even national TV. He often did so by tipping off blogs using fake email addresses and made up stories, creating news and buzz from basically nothing. When it comes to manipulating the media, he's the man. Or at least he used to be. His books are more of a warning about the fallacy of the media, and not tips on how to manipulate it.

"Blogs have enormous influence over other blogs, making it possible to turn a post on a site with only a little traffic into posts on much bigger sites, if the latter happens to read the former. Blogs compete to get stories first, newspapers compete to "confirm" it, and then pundits compete for airtime to opine on it. The smaller sites legitimize the newsworthiness of the story for the sites with bigger audiences. Consecutively and concurrently, this pattern inherently distorts and exaggerates whatever they cover."[4]

As church communicators, using tactics like this would force us to lie, gossip, cheat and maybe even steal. It certainly helps perpetuate the distribution of misinformation and fake news.

---

4 Excerpt From: Trust Me, I'm Lying: Confessions of a Media Manipulator by Ryan Holiday (Portfolio, 2013)

I'm certainly not making the case for doing anything shady or dishonest, but knowing how the system works can help you navigate it better when trying to get your story out there.

If anything, this proves that replying to the blogger who is writing a post about your church can be just as important as replying to the New York Times. Just because one is a major reputable news organization, and the other may very well be a guy in his pajamas working from his mom's basement, doesn't mean that what they write can't make waves in the community or even nationwide.

In today's world of tight deadlines and unreasonable quotas, reporters aren't taking the time they should be taking to verify sources or quotes. If a blogger publishes it, then they can quote the blogger and move onto the next story. No need to verify if the quote was written down correctly, learn more about the context, or verify if it was even said at all. If something needs to be corrected later, they'll just post an update to the story and blame the blogger. Never mind that most people will have already read the story, and no one will go back to read the update.

I've seen the New York Times, Washington Post, The Blaze, Daily Beast, and Huffington Post all quote me from posts by no name bloggers without ever reaching out to me to verify the quote or ask for more information. Sometimes they'll even re-publish the blog post word for word without writing a new story. It's quite amazing.

I find it remarkable that anyone with a laptop can now be a

reporter. These days anyone can write a blog post, and if the subject is good enough, it can be picked up and republished on Huffington Post or Daily Beast and attributed to you as if you're a real journalist with an editor and years of training. I applaud the advancement in technology. It's a crazy time to be alive with how much information is posted every day. But the cost of speed and efficiency has been quality control and fact checking. The high standards of journalism have taken a nose dive across the board. And the public is oblivious to it, or too busy to really care.

In the same way we buy food from the grocery store, or order food at a restaurant and trust that the government has done its job to regulate and protect us from harmful products and food handling practices, we blindly trust anything we read. At least at a restaurant we can check the latest heath rating and inspection report.

You've got to dig pretty deep these days to inspect a news story. Have you ever looked into who wrote that article you just read? How often do you click the links and dig deeper into the sources?

We read something online or in a newspaper and it just inherently comes across as fact. In the back of our minds we just assume we aren't being manipulated or lied to.

So don't brush off the local blogger as a nobody or a small opportunity, you never know who might pick up the story. And if they get something wrong, be quick to request changes before someone quotes it. Once it gets quoted, it can take on a life of its own. Then you're not only requesting changes from the source, but the ten other sites who all copied and pasted it. By the time it's all fixed (if it gets fixed) the bad information has already been read so many times and you've lost control of the story.

OTHER CHURCHES

Building relationships is something that should go well beyond just press and bloggers. It's important to build relationships everywhere you go. To build a better perception of your church, the more people who get to know you the better.

When it comes to other churches, remember we are all on the same team. Don't wall yourself off from other churches, or hold your best ideas for yourself. Don't just watch what other churches are doing from afar, seek to collaborate with them.

Invite other communications directors out to lunch, or over to your church to sit down with the team. If you just completed a really successful sermon series or marketing campaign - package it up and throw it online for free. Share it with your colleagues.

Again, the best way to build a great relationship with someone is to anticipate their needs and try to add value to their lives. If your church has something to share that can help other churches, then don't hold back on the generosity.

If you're a smaller church, don't criticize the big mega

church in town. This makes me so sad when I hear it. Every time you point out the weaknesses or differences in a big church in order to show the strengths of your church - that's just not loving, and it's not helpful. That's not how you want to grow your church.

One of the best ways to get to know people who do what you do, and build relationships with other churches, is to join one of the many church communications Facebook groups that are online. There can be a lot of noise to sort through from time to time, but there's also a lot to learn and plenty of opportunity to get to know your peers. You're not alone. There are thousands of people just like you, at churches like yours as well as churches bigger and smaller than yours.

YOUR COMMUNITY

Getting out into the community and meeting people outside your building should be a big priority for your church. God commanded us to "go and tell" but so much of what we do as a church is "come and see." Be active in your community and engage people where they are.

This means participating in community events, city-sponsored activities, restaurants, sports, and more. The more you can get out and meet people, as a church, the more they'll get to know the real you.

This is where a good branding strategy can also help maximize your PR efforts. Consider branded t-shirts, car decals, coffee mugs, signage, and other marketing materials that can help bring more visibility to your church and message.

A church that does a great job at this is Gwinnett Church in Sugar Hill, Georgia. They are a satellite campus of North Point Ministries, and led by Jeff Henderson. Even before the church launched and moved into its building, they would use the hashtag #FORGwinnett to spread their message. Even during construction of the building, the sign on the road just read "#FORGwinnett."

They also handed out car decals and t-shirts to just about every church goer, even during the early stages when they would meet at another church and in people's homes.

The idea is that the church as a whole has long been known for what we are against, and they want to be a church that is known for what they are for. Gwinnett is the county that the church serves, so they decided they want to be known for loving the community of Gwinnett. When people would see the sign on the road or people wearing the t-shirts, they'd either stop and ask what it was about or they'd look up the hashtag online.

The #FORGwinnett campaign has been a great way to start conversations, build relationships, and bring positive awareness not only about the church, but about what the church stands for.

Social media is also a great way to not only engage with your local community, but your broader online community as well. It can be one of the easiest ways to reach the majority of people in your area, or any area you want to target.

Start by engaging with the real people who follow you. Stop using Facebook and Twitter as just a platform for promotions and distributing content. Producing and posting great content is huge, but that has to only be part of your strategy.

You need to be listening to others and actively engaging in building relationships with people online. Don't be the church that just posts blog posts and announcement after announcement without any personality behind it, or without any engagement with the real people who are reading it. Share and retweet what others are posting. Interact with people in the comments. Show some love and respect for the people you're trying so hard to reach.

Let people get to know you and actually take the time to get to know them, because some day you might find yourself in a position where it's really important to clarify your message or correct a mistake, and you'll not only need people on your side but you'll want as many people as possible to actually listen to what you are saying and not just blow you off.

I can't emphasis enough how important this is. It's something that may seem like not a big deal now when things are going great. But when the time comes and you haven't put in the effort, it's going to come back and bite you.

LOCAL ORGANIZATIONS

You should also reach out to organizations in your area and take people out for coffee and lunch. Just get to know them and see how you can meet their needs.

The more people who know you in the community the better. Not only is it more people who can say "yeah I've heard of that church, I know the pastor, he's a great guy" but it also means if they come across a bad article on the church they'll read it with a bias that they know you're better than the media might be portraying you.

You should know and build relationships with local shelters, food banks, and non-profits in your area. There may be some impactful ways you can partner together, but at the very least you can support each other through prayer and get to know each other better based on your shared connection with the community.

Also think about the local restaurants and small businesses that would love to have closer ties with your congregation. Nowhere else in the community do you see groups of people gather on a regular basis like you do with churches. Whether you have 100 people attending your church each week, or 5000, that's value for a local small business.

Be careful not to turn your bulletin into a list of paid ads, and I definitely wouldn't ask your pastor to start wearing sponsors logos on his suit or hang a neon sign from the podium. But I don't see anything wrong with posting on Facebook that the local yogurt shop is offering 10% off after church, or that the local pizza joint is a favorite spot for staff meetings.

Too many churches are afraid to associate with

organizations that aren't from the church. It's really a shame.

THOUGHT LEADERS

One of the best ways to get people talking about you, is to get someone they already know and trust to start talking about you.

Identify celebrities, other high-profile pastors, business leaders, and anyone else with a little blue checkmark next to their name on Twitter and start building relationships with them.

A retweet here and there from someone with influence and reach can add a ton of credibility for you. The next time you send out a press release, including a quote from a thought leader outside of your organization will have a lot more pull than anything you wrote to include from your pastor.

Start by sharing their content, and engaging with them on social media. Reach out and email people to tell them how much you and your church admire them. It's not hard to make new friends, even famous ones. You just have to get out there and try.

PROXIMITY MATTERS

Keep in mind that when it comes to building authentic relationships, you can't automate the process or hide behind a screen. Healthy relationships rely on human interaction.

Have you ever made fun of someone, but then you meet them and you start to regret what you said? Maybe you still don't like them, but once you've made that human connection it changes things a bit.

That's because proximity matters. Any decent person responds positively to human interaction. You've really got to be calculated and intentional to be mean to someone to their face, but behind their back or in a comment on Facebook it takes little effort at all to be mean.

When someone is right in front of you and can see that they are human, that they have a past and a future. You can see that they are created in God's image just like you. You can see their expressions, and feel their warmth. It changes things.

Touch takes it a step further. Put you hand on someone's shoulder or elbow, and they'll instantly feel more trust between you. That's why the Bible tells us to lay hands on each other when praying, because there is power in that type of interaction. We are wired for it.

This matters because when people know you and are familiar with you, then they're more likely to give you the benefit of the doubt. This is important to think about when building relationships with anyone, especially reporters and people in the public outside your church.

If someone is going to write a negative article about you,

chances are the hit is going to be a bit softer if they know you or even if they've had some interaction with you. It's easy to write an article about someone whom you've never met and probably never will. But once you interact with them and you have a face and a memory attached to them, it makes it harder to be mean. Maybe you know a bit about their personal story, and have seen pictures of their kids. It changes the perspective and tone.

Get off the phone and away from your computer from time to time and make an effort to meet people for lunch and coffee. Do more video calls than phone calls. Visit businesses instead of just emailing them. If a reporter is doing a story on your church, invite them to church so they experience it first hand. Getting to meet people and shake their hand will have a much more lasting impact.

Now I'm not a baseball fan. I'm not even a sports fan. But I am a Jimmy Fallon fan. My wife and I will stay up late a lot of nights just watching YouTube clips of Fallon. Awhile ago I came across this clip where Jimmy Fallon was asking New York Yankees fans to boo Robinson Cano. Apparently, Cano left the Yankees for the Mariners for a $240 million contract and that upset a lot of Yankees fans.

Jimmy setup a big cardboard cutout of Cano on the streets of New York and gave people an opportunity to boo it. People had fun going off on this cardboard cutout, yelling obscenities and throwing things, and telling Cano how they really felt about him leaving.

What they didn't realize was the real Robinson Cano was hiding behind the cardboard cutout. As they were going off on the fake Cano, he would walk out and people would instantly change their attitude and demeanor.

Most people apologized and shook his hand, as they instantly became star struck. A moment ago they were cussing him out being as mean as they could be — but a moment ago he wasn't a real person, he was just cardboard. Now that he's a real person living and breathing in front of them, they show him the proper respect that any human deserves. His proximity to them changed their perception and their actions. One guy even said, "I still don't like what you did, but it's a pleasure to meet you and I'd love to shake your hand."

You need to get in front of the booing by building relationships and creating opportunities for people to get to know the real you. It can completely change the tone and message of any story about your church.

I've met with reporters and bloggers who wrote bad stuff about us, and completely turned around their perception of us (and my perception of them) just by meeting face to face and having a real conversation. I've de-escalated loud protests by offering coffee and shaking people's hands, even as they held signs calling me names.

As a PR person, at least a third of your time should physically be spent simply communicating with and fostering relationships with others.

Remember, PR is all about managing perception. The more people saying and thinking nice things about you the better.

It's the same game the media is playing with you. They know how to manipulate the public's perception in order to sell newspapers and get more clicks. Even the Christian media does this. Try reading an article on a Christian news site without closing four ads and panicking to find your mute button. They make their money off each page view just like every other news site.

If you aren't playing the game too, then you're going to lose by default. You've got to play, but you've got to play with integrity and kindness. That means actually get to know people because they are great people, not because you want to use them.

CHAPTER SIX

THE POWER OF THE PRESS

"When it comes to media relations it's not just about establishing a connection with a reporter. Maintaining a relationship over time will be the key to driving consistent results."

– Carol Lee, Tech Affect

As I said before, one of the most valuable and profitable relationships you can build is with the press. The press can be an intimidating force, but they can also be one of the most advantageous resources to getting the gospel to the masses. That's why you need a media relations plan.

I have found that when you actually take the time to get to know the men and women who are helping inform the public about the news, there are some wonderful people among them who love the Lord and love the church. Even most non-Christian reporters and journalists are genuinely interested in just reporting the facts, but they have so much working against them like deadlines and quotas that have changed the game.

It is definitely worth your time and resources to have an active plan in place to work with the press on an on-going basis, as well as to actively pitch stories about your church that might be relevant to the community.

A positive story about your church in the newspaper or on a popular website can help you reach the very audience that you should be trying to reach. In fact, besides social media, a great news story is one of the only ways to reach that audience, and to do so in a way that is meeting them where they already are.

With that said, I know there will still be some of you who want to argue back and forth on whether it's worth your time to pursue stories in newspapers and blogs. Perhaps you're a small church struggling with keeping your Facebook updated. You certainly can make a great argument for not having the resources to care about pitching press releases.

However, nothing you do or don't do is going to change the fact that you have no control over when a story about your church is going to break. If something newsworthy happens that affects or involves your church, you're going to wish you had been better prepared to deal with reporters calling your front desk or showing up to your church service with TV cameras.

And being prepared for when that happens has everything to do with building relationships and pitching stories, and less to do with communications plans and standard protocol (although both are very important).

This is when the phrase "a good defense is a good offense" is absolutely true. If you take the time and effort to build up a good perception of your church, it will soften the blow if something negative ever does come your way.

The relationships you've built with press and media contacts will not only come in handy if something negative comes out about your church - more on that later - but they will also be key in gaining visibility for the positive stories you wish to exploit.

You cannot wait around and expect people to write about the good things you are doing. You must tell them about it, and also give them reason to promote it for you when there is so much out there competing for their time.

Your PR plan should include your goals and processes for working with the media, as well as how and when you'll pitch them stories to promote what you are doing.

Pitching a story to the press can prove to be quite the art form. It should be well planned and thought out. If all you're doing is simply writing up press releases and blasting them out to the masses, then you're wasting a lot of valuable time.

Leverage your relationships to pitch the people you know directly. Every reporter has a short list of people they'll listen to first. They want to work with the people they trust and have relationships with, so they know the facts they get are straight and can easily be integrated into a story without the hassle of extensive research. Hardly ever do they need to pick from the stack of releases that come through every day, if they have enough trusted PR contacts ready to work with them.

When it comes time to pitching a story, there are certain things you want to get right. Reporters do not have the time to hunt down details, especially on a story that may not be a high priority for them. Put in the work, so they don't have to, and you'll have a better chance of getting your story published.

PITCHING A STORY

Email is the preferred method to pitch a story to a reporter. Some will argue that the best thing to do is pick up the phone, but I disagree. Email gives you the best option of getting all the pertinent information in their hands. If you have direct relationships with the press then you'll hardly ever need to use wire services to get a release out. Just email your contact directly.

I will say, once you know them personally it is definitely a good idea to send off a text message or pick up the phone to alert them about your email. But crafting that email well is the important part.

When emailing a reporter be sure to address them by name. And be sure you spell it correctly. The best pitch won't ever get read if you call Dave by the name of Dan, or if you assume Dana is a woman and not a man.

Know who you are addressing, and appeal to their interests. The writer who normally works the technology beat probably isn't going to care what your church is up to, unless of course you just developed an awesome new app.

Find the best writer who will be interested in the topic you are pitching. More often than not this will be the faith and religion reporter, or if at a TV station, the news reporter that covers your neighborhood.

Whether you have an existing relationship with this person or not, your email should start out with something that helps connect you to this person and elevates you above the rest of the people currently pitching them.

One of the best ways to do this is to research what they've written about lately, so you can reference it in your pitch. It shows you follow what they care about. Most reporters aren't sporadic in what they report on. Pick up on their thread and find a way for your story to fit into it. Don't hesitate to throw a little flattery and charm into it either.

Then get right to the point. Don't bury the lead, as they say. In no more than one or two sentences, explain what the story is about and why it's unique.

The remainder of your email pitch should include all the pertinent details of the story. The idea is to make it as easy as possible for them to write a unique article on the subject you are pitching. Think about their needs and try to meet them.

"PR is not advertising. Your pitch should be about the reporter and her publication's needs, not your own."

– Sean Lenehan, Voice Communications

There have been many times where I have included a fully written post, only to have a reporter cut and paste it in its entirety as their published article. It's a little surreal the first time you read an article you wrote published in a newspaper but attributed to someone else's name. It really makes you think twice about what you read.

Whether you choose to include a full article, or just the information they need to write their own, you must write in a way that makes it easy for them to cut and paste. The pronouns you use should be in the third person, as if the reporter is writing about the church (they, them, etc.).

One of the most important items you must include is a quote

from a relevant representative, preferably two. Again, the goal is to do as much of the work for them as possible. When they are able to include a quote in their article, it will have the appearance that they conducted an interview and did their research. It adds weight and validity to their article. More often than not, with tight deadlines and multiple article quotas per day, they don't have time to conduct lengthy interviews. Provide these details for them and you'll have a better chance of your article being published.

Make the quotes count. Typically, they'll want one from the senior pastor or whoever is the most well-known to the public. Whenever possible also include a quote from a church member, or another staff member. The idea is to make it look less like it was handed to them, and more like they actually did the work. Speed up your internal approval process by writing the quote yourself and getting your pastor to approve it or make quick changes if needed. I know, it seems disingenuous, and that's because it is. We're playing by their rules, not ours.

This all may seem shallow, but that is how the game is played these days. Your reporter will appreciate the help, and they'll reach out to you directly the next time they are fishing for a story. Why would they not want to work with you again, if you're the one who does all their work for them?

Also, be sure to include any additional facts and tidbits of information that are important to the story. You can list these out in bullet point form if needed. Don't assume they know how big your church is, or how to spell your pastor's name. Include things like when the church was planted, how many locations you have, and whatever else may be relevant to the story.

A lot of that information can be included in what is called a boiler plate paragraph. Typically, at the end of a press release you will include a single paragraph about the church that gives important information such as the proper name, address, contact info, number of locations, the mission statement, and more.

Even though you're including all of this information, you must keep the length of your email as short as possible. The entirety of your story should take no more than a single page if printed out. A typical news article is anywhere from 500 to 800 words in length. If you include more than that, they'll be overwhelmed and move on. If it's too short, they may not have the time to fill in the blanks.

You may also want to include photos or video clips that are relevant to the story. Every news article that is posted online will include at least one photo. If you don't provide one, then they are going to use the stock image they have on file for your church and chances are it's not going to be a flattering one. Provide them high quality professional photos that would work well for an article header.

I always kept a DropBox folder up to date with new images, and linked to it in our boiler plate description that went out with every pitch or reply to a reporter. The good ones would use them, while the ones bent on being negative would always prefer their grainy photos from the 90's that made us look like a cult. You can only do so much.

Lastly, you'll want to include an easy way for them to get a hold of you. Even if it's someone you talk to often, include your direct phone number, email, and even your Twitter handle in every correspondence.

These people are working from their cars, from coffee shops, and news vans. They don't have assistants anymore. Most of my communications with the reporters I knew happened over text message and Twitter direct messages.

INTERVIEWING TIPS

Whether a story you pitched is picked up, or a reporter reached out to you for comment on something they are already writing, there may come a time where you'll be interviewed.

Most members of the press do not want to run a factually incorrect story. Even when dealing with an aggressive journalist, it can be helpful to remember that they may treat the "other side of the story" just as aggressively in pursuit of unbiased truth.

Problems occur when they don't get an accurate story from one side. I like to think that back in the day this would mean they wouldn't run the story if they didn't have all the information, but I don't know if that's true. For as long as I've been alive, if they want to run a story, they'll do it with or without you.

That's why it's important to respond to journalists and

reporters, and to be prepared with your side of the story at all times. It's up to you, and you alone, to get your story out there, and to do your best to help them understand it. If they get it wrong, chances are that's on you.

Journalists are usually interested in offering a different angle on the story that includes fresh information or better evidence than what they already have. Especially if it's something that others are going to report on as well. They need to stand out and be unique.

There may come a time when you are chosen as a spokesperson for your church, either in writing or over the phone or on camera.

Your church will be ideally positioned to the press when your spokesperson sticks to the approved messaging and follows these basic principles:

PREPARE FOR YOUR INTERVIEWS

The journalist is going to be prepared for the interview, even if they are pretending that they aren't. So don't walk into an interview not knowing what you are going to say.

It's ok to request the reporter to send you their questions in advance. PR pros may disagree with me on that, but in my experience, you have nothing to lose and everything to gain. Most of the time they won't have the time to do this, as they're always hustling and working on the fly. But every once in a while, you get lucky and that heads up will help you prepare better. When it comes down to it, they want to produce a good news story, not quote some fumbling un-prepared guy who works at a church.

ANTICIPATE THE QUESTIONS

Whether you get the questions ahead of time or not, take time to think about the questions you might be asked, then prepare your answers in advance.

Once you have your answers written out, then try to simplify them as much as possible. Get your answers down to just a few key points, and memorize them. Your key points should be short enough to tweet, and you should try to work them into every answer if possible.

PRACTICE MOCK INTERVIEWS

Ask a friend or co-worker to pretend to be a reporter so you can practice saying your answers. Don't let the first time you are saying them be on camera.

This can sometimes feel weird or you don't have the time, so I'd often record myself saying the answers out loud. Being able to play back the recording helps you listen from a different perspective. I'd often make changes to my wording or tone based on how I sounded on the recording.

MAKE YOURSELF ACCESSIBLE

Don't hide your contact information, or ignore your phone. When a reporter calls, respect that they are under a deadline and be available to them.

Most reporters don't have much time to wait on you. While they would prefer a direct quote and new information, they don't need it to run their story. You'll usually have between one and six hours to generate your response and get it back to the reporter before they have to publish.

If you aren't prepared to answer their questions when they request them, then let them know what is going on. It's ok to say "I'm planning on getting you a statement, we just need another hour." If they know they'll get a statement from you, more often than not they will wait for it or they'll let you know when their hard deadline is.

If you don't communicate with them, they are more likely to go ahead without you, which probably won't work out positively for you. This is what happens when you read something like, "Representatives from the church were not available for comment." in articles. That looks like you refused to answer or didn't care, when in reality it could have just meant you were in a meeting when they called.

KEEP ANSWERS SHORT BUT INFORMATIVE

Don't ramble on. Keep your answers directly related to the

question. If you can't answer them in one or two sentences, then they aren't going to use that answer. You'll either be quoted without the context you provided, or you won't be quoted at all.

Try writing out your answer beforehand, then keep taking words out until you've reduced it down to the plain and simple point you are trying to make.

They are looking for quick sound bites. Whether you are being interviewed for TV or for an article, the quotes that will make it are going to be the short and pithy ones. Don't lose the opportunity by talking too much.

RESPECT THEIR TIMELINES

Again, they will publish without you. Most reporters are working on two to three stories a day. They don't have time to wait, or do proper research. They're not even looking to hear your whole story. They're looking for a couple sound bites to make it look like they interviewed someone, and then they can move onto the next story.

When they call and say they're doing a story, you've got to drop what you're doing and kick it into gear if you want to be a part of it.

CORRECT MISINFORMATION

You'll be misquoted. Names will get spelled wrong. Critical information will be missing from the story even though you said it ten times. That's just how the game is played. Most of the time it's an honest mistake. The reporter is in a hurry and things get sloppy or were simply misunderstood.

Unfortunately, once a story is out, people read it or watch it, then they move on. Nobody goes back to see if anything changed.

But it's still important for you to work with the reporter to get the correct information out there. Follow up in an email or a phone call, and stay persistent. If you need to, find out who the editor is and work with them on making the correction. Chances are the reporter is out in the field and onto the next story, so it could take them days to update it. But an editor is chained to a desk and can make it happen quicker, and is likely to care more about getting the facts straight. After all, that's their job.

This is vitally important in case the story gets picked up by other news sites or bloggers. They'll start quoting the original story, and if the information is incorrect, then you'll lose control of it forever. Even if you track every instance down and get them all corrected, you can't change the perspective of all the people who have already read it.

ASK FOR CLARIFICATION

One way you can avoid misinformation getting out there, is to ask clarifying questions. If you don't understand what is being asked of you, request that they ask it in a different way or explain it to you. Remember, they're just looking for a sound byte. They won't air or quote the conversations back and forth between the two of you.

If you aren't sure that they understood your answer, ask them to repeat it to you so you can be sure they got it right. If you show them respect, they'll work with you to get the story right. Their reputation is on the line too.

THINK BEFORE YOU SPEAK

It's ok to pause. If you're on camera, your entire interview isn't going to be presented unless of course you are live. And if you're talking to a newspaper reporter, they aren't going to report your pauses or describe you as slow. If you need a minute to think through your answer, take your time. As much as you can, avoid "um's' and "uh's," but it's perfectly acceptable to be silent for a second. They will wait for your answer.

It's better than blurting out something you didn't mean to blurt out. Because once it's out, it's out.

REPEAT YOUR CORE MESSAGE

Repetition is key. Get your key points out there as many times as possible. They are more likely to air or print something you repeated several times.

In fact, try to come up with one or two key points, and work that point into every single answer you give them. Remember, the entire interview isn't going to be aired. They are only going to air one of your answers, so you're not going to look weird repeating yourself. But if you have the same answer to every question, chances are pretty good that your point is going to get some air time.

It's also not in their best interest to plug your website for you. If you repeat it several times, you'll have a better chance of it making it into the story.

NEVER SAY "NO COMMENT"

If there's a question you want to avoid, or something you don't have permission to answer, try to redirect it back to your main point instead.

If you say, "no comment" or "I can't answer that" then it makes you sound guilty and that you have something to hide. They'll air that for sure, and you'll end up looking bad even though you didn't say anything at all.

When you say, "I can't answer that," it makes it look like you've been handled and that there is something to hide. It also gives them the impression that you aren't the person they should be talking to, and may make a big mess for yourself when they try to go above your head to get the real story.

Instead say things like "I don't have an answer on that right now, but I'll get back to you on that." This buys you more time to come up with an answer, and worse case you follow up with an email that says, "I'm sorry I wasn't able to get any more information on that at this time." They aren't going to be waiting for your answer anyway.

DON'T SPECULATE

Share what you know and commit to finding out what you don't know. It's not your job to give your opinion. You're representing the church and need to stick to the talking points that you prepared.

If they ask you something you weren't prepared for, just share what you do know and if you aren't sure, say something like "I'm not sure about that but I'll find out for you."

You can then follow up in an email once you find out what to say. But again, they'll likely have moved on without including that part. When I have used that line I've never once had a reporter follow up and ask if I found out the answer. They just skip it.

What you don't want to do is panic and think you have to have an answer for everything.

DON'T LOSE YOUR COOL

It's important to stay calm and collected. Sometimes they'll try to get under your skin. After all, controversy sells, so if they get you worked up, then it makes for a better story.

If they've said something to upset you, or they're pushing your buttons, just pause and take a breath. Stick to your points, and continue to repeat yourself.

It's really important to smile the entire time. Don't squint your eyes and look annoyed. If you do, you can be sure that will be the still shot that goes up on the blog later.

DON'T USE CHURCH JARGON

Remember that non-Christians are going to see this or read about it, and that it may end up being a great opportunity for them to be exposed to your church. Don't turn them off or confuse them by using internal language, or language that only Christians would understand.

Things like "loving on," "doing life with," "sanctuary," "life groups," "sacraments," etc. are things that no one is going to understand.

If you're talking about small groups, try to briefly explain what they are, such as "small groups are where people in the church gather in each other's homes throughout the week to share a meal and get to know each other better."

If you normally call your worship space a "sanctuary," for the purpose of the interview just call it an "auditorium." Think of the end viewer or reader, who may be an unbeliever who is interested in coming to your church. Make it super easy to understand.

DON'T TRY TO STOP A STORY

Never try to stop a member of the press from running a story. Offer to help with the story instead. It will never end well if you're trying to stop a story from coming out. If they're already inquiring about it, then your best bet is to become a part of the story so you can do your best to get your side right.

Offer to connect them with the right people they need to interview. Provide the info they need for their research. Chances are if you provide it, they'll use it rather than digging deeper.

DON'T SAY ANYTHING "OFF THE RECORD"

Remain professional with the press at all times. Even if you've come to be friends with a reporter. There really is no such thing as "off the record." If it's good, chances are they'll find a way to work it into the story one way or the other. Most reporters feel it is their sworn duty to report something they know about. Just because you said it off the record doesn't mean they can't ask a church member or another staffer to verify it on the record, and then quote them instead.

Any respectable journalist will abide by the off the record rules if you make it clear up front that you are off the record, but when it comes down to it, there's nothing legally binding about the words.

Also keep in mind that bloggers don't have a boss or editor

looking over their shoulder, so they have no obligation to adhere to journalistic standards. You never know what they'll write, and just because they don't quote you doesn't mean they won't share their opinion on something you said in order to get the information out there.

DON'T SAY ANYTHING YOU WOULDN'T WANT TO READ IN THE STORY LATER

Don't get sidetracked out of the key issue. Bring it back to the core message if you need to.

Never made bad jokes or lose professionalism. Remember that the entire time you are with the reporter, they are paying attention to your conversation. Even after the interview is over and you've turned to chit chat, your words can be used in the story. In fact, they'll often use opportunities like that to catch you off your guard.

I learned that lesson the hard way. We were making a bid for a huge building that was for sale near our main church campus. The building and property was a perfect fit to expand our church's central operations and main auditorium. It was right off the public transportation line, and in the middle of a proposed mixed-use development that was supposed to be the new epicenter of the city. It was exactly what we had been looking for, and at the end of the day it was the only option we found that was big enough to fit our growing congregation.

We needed to expand and this building was the only option

within the city. There wasn't a lot of undeveloped space in the area, and there are a lot of restrictions on new buildings, particularly worship centers. It's not like down South where you can just buy an empty field and build a massive auditorium to your specs.

We made an offer on the building, more than they were asking, and the owner accepted it. Unfortunately, the city turned out to have a claim on the property, as it was one of several locations they had the right to seize while they planned a new maintenance facility for the mass transit train line. Even though our offer was accepted, the city blocked the sale.

The hardest part was the property would sit vacant for up to five years while the city decided if they even needed it. They wouldn't be ready to build their maintenance facility for several years, but they seized about five different properties while they determined which one they might use. If they didn't choose this one, they'd end up selling it at auction, but that could be five to seven years later and we didn't have that kind of time.

We tried working with the city to show them that our church would be better for the community than a maintenance yard, especially since they had several other properties that were a great fit for their new facility, but we only had the one option for the growth of our church. I appeared at every public hearing they held for months, and spoke our concerns but they wouldn't budge on their decision, nor would they work with us to find another suitable location for the church. Eventually they stopped letting me speak on the matter.

There were no legal options we could pursue, and our efforts to work with them were failing. We felt we had no other choice than to try the matter in the court of public opinion so we started a website to draw attention to the situation and get the public's interest. After all, even non-Christians could agree that a beautiful church campus that doubles as a public auditorium, book store and cafe, was a better option in the up and coming shopping district than an ugly maintenance yard for trains.

A local TV station quickly picked up on the story and sent a reporter out to interview me. The whole thing lasted 30 minutes. I hit every talking point we worked up, and was so excited that they were devoting that much time to the story. I knew they'd take a controversial angle with it - pitting the big rich mega-church up against the city who was just trying to support the popular mass transit line. But I had high hopes. The reporter seemed genuinely interested, was friendly and asked great questions.

What I didn't expect is the reporter baiting me into a corner as I walked him out to their news van. With the interview over, but the camera apparently still recording audio, he asked me, "Do you think God wants you to have this building?"

My response, with my guard down and thinking he and I were now buddies, was "Sure, we believe God wants us to have this building. We wouldn't be pursuing it if we didn't."

Dang it. Why did I say that? As they hopped into their van and sped off, I was praying the cameraman didn't capture me saying that. Sure enough, when the evening news came on that night, the lead story was "Local church says we believe God wants us to have this building!" with my photo next to it.

Thirty minutes of interview, and the only clip they aired was audio of me saying those words. They didn't even air him asking the question. It played as if I volunteered the information. None of the context was included. Not a single key point made it into the story. The whole thing was about how the wacky megachurch thought they could take someone else's property just because God told them to.

I should have said something like, "Well I'm not God, I don't know what he wants. But I do know that we love this community and want to continue being a part of it, but this building is the only option we have to expand our growing church. If the city continues to block the sale so they can sit on the property for five years then we'll have to move more than 150 jobs and a place of worship for 5000 church members to another city."

Even my co-workers the next morning in the church office were asking me why I would say such a thing. It was a nightmare.

The city issued a statement the next day saying that they don't just give up buildings because a church says God wants them to have it. Man, I envied the city PR guy. He had me and he knew it. We lost control of the message, and the public turned against us.

A reporter caught me off-guard and it threw a whole building campaign off the tracks. We might have been able to recover by doing another interview and explaining what happened. I certainly wanted to stay in the fight. Unfortunately, I didn't get the chance to even clarify my position because the prevailing decision was to move on. We were already under a lot of pressure at the time, and frankly it marked the beginning of us giving up on the future of the church. In hindsight, we would have been selling that building a year later had we known the church would soon close.

I don't share this story to scare you into never talking to a reporter. I share it because it's a good lesson to always stick to your talking points, and always be on guard when talking to a reporter - especially one you don't have an existing relationship with.

I also hope it's a good lesson in not giving up. Whenever possible, clarify what you meant to say. Try to correct your missteps. In my opinion, we owed it to the public to share what happened and what we really meant.

We let their poor perception of the church linger, and frankly that hurt churches everywhere and it hurt the people who followed the story. It pains me to think that I helped justify hatred for the church in a lot of people who just needed one more reason to stay away. I regret that we didn't keep fighting to get our message out there. We may not have ever won the building, but we could have helped correct the perception of the church.

HOLDING A PRESS CONFERENCE

Lastly, I want to touch on one technique of working with the press that a lot of churches don't use. There may come a time when hosting a press conference is necessary to get the word out about a big announcement, or to respond to something major.

Rather than interviewing with that TV station about our church building that I shared with you earlier, I wish we had done a press conference where we could have controlled the story better.

Press conferences are certainly a rare occurrence with churches, but I think that is a shame. I believe it is because most churches are unprepared with how to hold one. They can be a great way to entice hype or get the word out fast about an important story. In times when you are responding to something negative, it can be a great way to show vulnerability as well as ensure that all new agencies receive the same information at the same time.

Certainly, press conferences should be reserved for big announcements and items that are definitely news worthy. Don't burn bridges with your media contacts by inviting them to an announcement about how you collected 500 coats for a coat drive. Nobody cares - that could have been handled in an email if it's important for you to get it out there. Press conferences are for big announcements such as major milestones, big building campaigns, major leadership changes, responses to a major crisis, or something that has a big impact on the community.

You can hold a press conference in your church auditorium, in your foyer, or even a public space. Wherever is the easiest to access and provides a great photo opportunity.

To get the word out you'll want to personally invite your press contacts. It may also be wise in this case to prepare a simple press release that goes out to all relevant media outlets. You may also want to post about it on social media, as well as your website or blog. Don't leave them hanging on the subject matter. Give them enough details so they'll be interested in attending, but hold back your best parts for the main event.

I highly suggest that anytime you make a major announcement via the press, you first inform your church. Whether it be just your members or key players, or the entire congregation, it is generally best practice to inform the people of your church first. This is particularly true if what you are announcing is in any way negative.

Your people will be waiting for answers, and they deserve to hear them from you and not from a press conference or from an article they read in the local newspaper. Because of this, you may want to time your press conference directly after a member's meeting or even a church service.

Kill two birds with one stone and invite the press into your members meeting so everyone hears it at the same time. This also has the added benefit of ensuring that no matter what is reported, your key people heard it the same way the reporters did and will be able to compare what was said verses what gets reported.

You can be sure that reporters will bring photographers and video crews to a press conference, so have this in mind. Be mindful of the setting and how it will look on TV. Provide a backdrop or stage setup that is attractive. Ensure that there is room for everyone to setup cameras so they get a good shot of the speaker. Make sure they have power and wifi access.

This is also a great opportunity to provide loving hospitality. Make it a joy to visit your church. Treat them like you treated the affluent new family that visited last Sunday. Put out water bottles, fresh coffee, snacks, and anything else that will make your guests more comfortable.

When you invite the press into your house, you can expect things to get a little pushier than you'll be used to. Everyone is getting the same information at the same time, so they'll be digging for unique angles that will make their article or TV spot stand out among the others.

Think about providing time for one on one interviews with you or the pastor, or any other spokesperson that would be relevant to the story. You invited them, so be accessible and accommodating. At the very least provide them with a final print out that includes every necessary detail for the story.

Follow up with every press contact and thank them for

coming, and share your regrets with those who didn't make it. Then provide them with all the details again. This also give you a chance to clarify anything you felt was unclear or got muddled. They'll be rushing to get a story out, and will appreciate having the facts and key points already written up for them.

CHAPTER SEVEN

THE POWER OF SOCIAL MEDIA

"Social media is changing the way we communicate and the way we are perceived, both positively and negatively. Every time you post a photo, or update your status, you are contributing to your own digital footprint and personal brand."

- Amy Jo Martin

The most effective way you can communicate with the public and shape the perception of your church, is through social media. It should be the most vital piece of your PR plan and overall communications strategy.

Social media is also an incredible tool to fulfill the mission of your church in ways you'll never be able to from the pulpit.

With a few key strokes, you can reach the nations with the message of your church, and you don't even have to raise support for missions.

There's nothing wrong with missions of course. But in today's world of social media, there is tremendous opportunity available to you at home, and most churches aren't fully taking advantage of it.

If your church loves people, then you should love social media. Jesus' last commandment to his disciples was to "be my witnesses in Jerusalem and in all Judea and Samaria, and to the end of the earth.[5]"

These days, our entire world is connected through social media. Facebook is "the end of the earth" because it's one way we truly are able to "make disciples of all nations.[6]" Those nations are on Facebook, as well as Twitter, Instagram,

---

[5] "But you will receive power when the Holy Spirit has come upon you, and you will be my witnesses in Jerusalem and in all Judea and Samaria, and to the end of the earth." - Acts 1:8 ESV

[6] "Go therefore and make disciples of all nations, baptizing them in the name of the Father and of the Son and of the Holy Spirit, [20] teaching them to observe all that I have commanded you. And behold, I am with you always, to the end of the age." - Matthew 28:19-20 ESV

Pinterest, Snapchat, and every other social media network.

As Christians, our biggest mission is to share the gospel of Jesus Christ with as many people as possible, and social media is a mission field populated with actual people who need the gospel. Our job is to make the gospel the hero of every post and get out of the way.

Jesus said Christians are the light of the world. The world is now on social media and Jesus loves every man and woman on social media sites, the popular sites and the not-so-popular ones. Therefore, churches should be using social media to point people to Jesus.

We can't do that if we are only posting about events and announcements. We can do so much better than that. There are rich opportunities to build relationships and get to know people on an intimate level.

There are 168 hours in a week. When you think about it, a church typically only engages with people for about an hour once per week. And it's all one-way communication. Sure, people may connect in small groups and with other ministries throughout the week, but my point is that there are typically 167 hours a week that your people are not engaging with your church.

Historically, there hasn't been anything we can do about that, but social media has totally changed the game. We know that people are spending nearly an hour every day scrolling through Facebook status updates, liking Instagram posts, or chatting on Messenger[7]. That's another 7 hours per week that you can get in front of them and engage with them.

They are sharing their most intimate thoughts, they are checking in at their favorite restaurants and posting pictures of what they are eating. They are cataloging milestones, and capturing every moment of their children's lives. If you pay attention, they are telling you and showing you how to minister to them with every post.

Social media is not just another advertising platform or activity for your interns to play around with. It's an investment in people. You can leverage it in a number of different ways to actually connect with people, whether they be volunteers, parents, new people who just visited your church, or people who have never been. It's an opportunity to invite people, and to equip others to invite their friends.

It used to be said that the parking lot of your church should be considered just as important as your front door. The idea being that as people drive up to your church for the first time, they already start to develop an opinion and feeling about their experience. Developing a welcoming parking process, keeping the grounds clean and beautiful, and providing helpful signage, are all some ways you can help people feel loved from the second they hit your property.

While that is still very true, the internet and social media has added a new layer. These days, before people ever consider

---

[7] Source: Business Insider: http://www.businessinsider.com/how-much-time-do-people-spend-on-facebook-per-day-2016-4

the possibility of visiting your church they are looking at your website and your social media platforms to get a feel for what your church is like.

They want to know if the people who attend your church are like them or not. They want to know what you believe, and if your actions actually match up with what you say you believe. They want to get a sense for whether they will belong, and whether they would be proud of ashamed to be seen there.

More practically they also want to know what it's like to check their kids into the nursery or kid's ministry area. For someone who has never been to a church, the whole idea of handing off their kids to some strangers is a scary thought. *What are they going to do for an hour? What are they going to teach my kids — I'm not even sure if I believe in Jesus yet, so are they going to force that on my child?*

Social media provides an opportunity to help answer those questions, not only by pointing to the resources and content you have made available, but by opening up a channel where you can connect person to person and walk them through their concerns and questions.

I have seen so many churches who publish posts that say something like "We can't wait to see you this Sunday," but then they don't have anyone responding to comments or messages that may come in. I've managed Facebook on Sundays for many churches, and people will frequently ask questions via Facebook Messenger. I had one guy who messaged a church's Facebook page to ask which exit to get off on the freeway. He was driving to church and needed directions. Had no one been manning the Facebook page that day, it's possible he would have never made it. Not only did he get directions in real time, but before he even hit the parking lot he was already developing a positive perception about the people of the church.

Had no one responded to him, he may have still found his way, but he probably would have felt ignored. Not a great way to make a first impression.

To this day I still hear so called social media experts and consultants tell people that social media is still so new and we are all just trying to figure this thing out together. But that doesn't add up anymore. As of this writing, social media has been around for nearly fifteen years, and while it continues to grow and evolve, I think that has more to do with the medium than it does the length of time it has been available. Social media is ever changing and always will be.

It's a communication method, a series of tools to help us connect with each other better. And as with any type of communication tool, you need to evolve and continue to be creative when using them to effectively market a product or service.

Where the church continues to fail, at least in general, is they see it as another advertising channel such as direct mail, billboards, radio, TV, or even email. Those methods are all one-way, and that used to be all we had.

Before the internet and social media, advertising and

marketing was exclusively about selling products. It wasn't relational. There was no way for the consumer to give feedback or express an opinion. TV, radio, and newspapers told us how to feel and what to buy. None of that is true anymore. The rules have completely changed.

Sure, social media can certainly be used to advertise and promote, but it's so much more than that. It is an entirely different thing all together.

Young people get this because they don't ever remember a time when there wasn't the internet and social media. There is a whole community of people who don't know the difference between offline and online because for them they have always overlapped and been intertwined. Churches that are still holding onto their sacred old school ways are struggling to even understand this, let alone adapt to it or capitalize on it.

It's time to wake up. Stop with the excuses. Ignore the old way of doing things, and embrace the fact that the rules have changed. If you don't understand it, hire someone who does. The opportunity to reach real people and point them to Jesus is too great to dismiss it.

I think it's ironic when I meet with churches who spend millions of dollars sending people on missions trips all over the world, but then tell me they don't see the value in spending a few thousand dollars a year on social media. If you gave me a million dollar budget for Facebook ads, I guarantee you that I'd be able to reach more people and more countries per year than your missions team. But the reality is, on Facebook you can do that without spending any money at all. If you want to accelerate your potential reach with Facebook ads, it's still only going to cost you a few hundred dollars to do it well. Even $50 on Facebook can help you reach a few thousand people.

I know I pick on missions trips and that upsets people. Don't get me wrong, I think missions are a great use of church funds. So, let's pick on church bulletins instead. I know just as many churches that are wasting money on printing bulky handouts every Sunday that no one reads. Printing these things on the church photocopier isn't that expensive, but when you calculate the time and energy it takes for someone on your staff to put the thing together, it adds up pretty quickly. And for very little payoff.

Whether it's the Communications Manager or the church secretary who puts the bulletin together, consider utilizing their time to better manage your Facebook and Twitter accounts. Use the money you spend on printing to run some Facebook ads instead.

I would love it if you just humored me and tried an experiment. Wait until your bulletin stock is all used up, then for the next six weeks stop printing it. You have to stick with it for six weeks because you are definitely going to get some push back the first week. Then a little pushback the second week. Then you'll suddenly find that no one is asking about the bulletin anymore. By the fourth or fifth week no one will care. Then you can look at the data. Did attendance change? Did people forget about important events? Chances are not much of anything will have changed, and you now have a case for stopping the bulletin permanently.

If I'm wrong, then I just gave you a six week break from what is most likely one of the most mundane parts of your job. Go back to printing it if it works for you. However, the churches I know who have taken this challenge have never returned to printing a bulletin. In fact, one church was able to sell their photocopier.

What you may notice during your six week bulletin experiment is that you'll get more questions on social media about events and registration. That's what you want. Because now you can engage with those people rather than communicating with them through a piece of paper.

The point of the experiment is to prove that you do have the time and resources to manage social media well, and maybe even do some paid ads. You just need to prioritize what you are spending your time and resources on. Why spend so much time and effort on bulletins, when you can accomplish the same thing through social media but with higher quality and greater returns? Why spend millions on overseas missions so people can have an experience, when you can reach every nation in the world through the content you post and conversations you have online?

If you're a larger church maybe you can do it all. I know plenty of churches who do social media well, have a large missions budget, and still print a bulletin. Do what works for you, but don't give up on the potential of social media just because you didn't try to do it well.

So how do you move from using social media as a billboard, to using it as a communications tool that helps you build a better perception for your church and reach your organizations goals?

ENGAGE WITH YOUR COMMUNITY

Social media should be conversational. It's not so much about what you post, but how you interact and engage with people.

Rather than posting about your church and what you offer, ask more questions that lead to conversations and create opportunities to point people to Jesus.

The best way to build up engagement — people commenting and interacting with you — is to start engaging. If that sounds like it was way obvious, it's because it is. You don't go to a party, sit in the corner and don't talk to anyone, then complain how everyone was unfriendly. Ask questions. Move around a bit. Introduce yourself. Dance!

When you ask questions, and expect your audience to engage, you have to engage back. Acknowledge their participation with a like, a reply comment, or a share. You can't ask them a question, or ask them to share a photo, and then never participate in the discussions or acknowledge the effort they made. If you don't engage back then the perception you are creating is that you clearly only care about getting likes.

BE STRATEGIC WITH THE CONTENT YOU SHARE

What you share speaks volumes about what is important to you, and what you want to be important to others.

When you post content, don't just share church related posts. In one of the church communications Facebook groups that I am a part of, a young woman asked the group if they thought it would be appropriate for her church to share about a missing girl in their community. She wasn't sure if it was appropriate because it wasn't a "church related post" and she wasn't even sure if the missing girl had any association with the church.

I and many others suggested that this is the exact type of thing you should be posting about from your church social media platforms. A little girl is missing in your community! If the church can't get involved in that because they're too busy posting about the next bake sale, then something is very wrong.

The best way to know what to post, is to first get to know who you are posting for. Do you have a target audience and goal in mind when you post, or are you simply checking off the list of things each ministry needs to communicate?

GET TO KNOW YOUR AUDIENCE

These days in order to sell a product, you can't just talk about how great it is and expect people to buy it. You have to put your product aside, and start thinking about the consumer directly.

Successful marketers will appeal to a buyer's needs, and convince them that their product solves their problem. Starbucks isn't just a great cup of coffee, it's a great place to hang out and meet with others besides the home or the office. The iPhone isn't just the best phone on the market, it's an extension of who you are and how connect with your friends, your business, and the world. If you voted for Obama, you weren't voting for a man, you were voting for change. All of these brands know how to appeal to their audiences needs and desires, and not just focus on how great their product is.

The main focus of a church isn't to sell products, but the buyer-first marketing concept can be applied just the same. Rather than focusing on your next event, or your great worship service, you need to focus on the people first, and create content and messaging that appeals to their interests and needs.

Instead of "Don't miss this week's message," try something like, "We'd love to see you this weekend. You'll feel like you finally found a place where you can belong," might appeal more to your audience's desires.

You can learn what they want by listening to what they are saying. When someone likes your page or comments on a post, click over to view their profile. Who are they? Where are they? What type of stuff do they post? Are they married? Kids? Conservative or liberal?

Within a minute or so you could easily be able to classify that person in at least one or two ways. This is very much like creating personas and target audiences, if you're at all familiar with those marketing tactics.

One of the most important categories you could place someone in is whether they are a current member, or potential member. Or do they live too far to ever be a member?

You can also easily pick up on how they talk, so you can start to use the same words and phrases that they use in your posts and comments.

Also look for what websites they frequently share, including news sites, magazines, and blogs. That will help you start to generate a list of sites that you could possibly share content from. If a large part of your audience reads and shares posts from Harvard Business Review, then maybe you can find some relevant posts to share from that site as well. Or maybe recipes and cat videos are more their flavor, then it should become yours too.

Use all of this information to know more about who you are reaching, and what they may want to see, or need to see, in their news feed. Craft your content around their needs not yours.

You may find that you have several different categories of people who follow and engage with your church. That's OK. That's totally to be expected. And there's nothing wrong with crafting content to reach each group. This is where an editorial calendar may come in handy so you know what type of content is going out and when.

When people start to feel like they know you, and you know them, then they'll more easily be able to convert into a visitor, and a member, and a donor... or more importantly, a disciple of Jesus Christ. Remember that people generally convert to community before they convert to Christ.

It takes time. You have to play the long game. Think of it like dating. Would you walk up to a pretty girl for the first time and ask her to marry you right off the bat? No, you'd introduce yourself. You'd maybe buy her a drink or ask her to share a meal. You'd ask her questions about herself and get to know her. After a few dates, you earn each other's trust and you decide whether you really like each other. Then comes a kiss, then marriage, then kids, then a boat. You know how it goes.

My point is, don't expect to post about your next event and expect everyone to just sign up. Most of them probably don't even know you, have never visited before, and don't know if they can even trust you. You're coming off as the creepy guy who's moving too fast. Get to know them first before you go asking everything of them.

MEASURE WHAT MATTERS

One of the great things about the internet and social media is that everything can be tracked and measured. When you post something, Facebook, Twitter, Instagram and every other social network will automatically track things for you such as how many people liked it, how many people shared it, how many people watched your video, etc. You can also measure how many people like your profile page, thus increasing your potential audience for the next post. Then there's things like reach - how many people your post could potentially show up in front of, and impressions - how many people actually saw it.

It can be incredibly satisfying to watch those numbers grow and grow the more active you become on social media. Likewise, it can be very frustrating and depressing when they don't grow. Or when you post something that you know is important, only to find hardly anyone saw it.

When I ask churches what their social media goals are, I hear things like "We want to have 5,000 page likes by the end of the year," or "We need to get 100,000 page views on our website by Easter."

The problem is, those goals rarely match up with the church's goals or vision. When I ask what the goals of the church are, I hear things like "We want to be a church where the un-churched and de-churched love to attend," or "We want to be known for serving our community." I even hear things like "We want to grow our attendance numbers to 3,000," or "We need to increase the number of regular donors by 10%."

Typically, that increase in traffic or increase in social media likes isn't necessarily going to translate to your church's goals. So why are you spending so much time worrying about how many people liked the last post if it isn't putting more butts in seats on Sunday, and it isn't converting your regular attenders into regular givers?

You need to align your communications goals with the

goals of the church.

Instead of reporting on how many likes you have, try creating a report that shows the different demographics and personas of the people you are reaching. Then show how many people in your audience you learned something new about based on what they are posting and conversations you've had with them through comments and messages. Show how many people got a direct invite to church, or how many people you helped by answering questions about the church. Show how many of your church members shared a post and included an invite to come to church on their own Facebook. Share stories more than you share likes.

You get the picture. Align the things you are tracking with the goals of the church, and you'll be able to better track how your efforts are actually affecting the bottom line (meaning attenders, members, donations, etc.).

Focus on engagement, learn about your audience and craft content that puts people first, then measure your success against your organization's goals not just your department's goals. Follow those principles and social media will end up being one of the best tools for shaping your church's perception, and getting your true message out to as many people as possible.

THE IMPORTANCE OF A SOCIAL MEDIA POLICY

Part of your social media strategy should include the use of a social media policy. This can be a controversial move for many people, but it can be incredibly useful to not only protect the church, but also to help align everyone with your mission. And more importantly, align the public's perception with your vision and goals.

A social media policy is a written document of guidelines and policies that can either be suggested or enforced, depending on what is needed and acceptable within your organization.

Typically, this is a document that would be placed into an employee manual, or included in on-boarding training for staff and volunteers.

It's simply a document of written guidelines suggesting how to act and interact with people on social media, so that your church is always seen in the best possible light. Remember that everything we say or do (or don't say and don't do) is PR. It all adds to the overall perception that people have of us as a person, of us as Christians, and by extension, how they feel about the church you represent.

The most common objection I hear to social media policies like this is that your employer, even a church, can't control what I do or post on my own personal channels or on my own personal time. First Amendment rights and all that. While that's legally true (it's actually a gray area, but I'm no lawyer), it doesn't mean the church can't provide some direction on what the best biblical behavior should be.

It's also good for a church, or any employer, to set exceptions in writing so everyone is on the same page. They may not be able to control what you post, but they certainly can fire you if what you post is shining a bad light on the church or dividing people from the core message.

Hopefully working for your church isn't just a job for you. I don't know why anyone would choose to work at a church just to check a job off their list. Certainly, the stress and lack of income isn't worth it. If you just want a low paying, low reward job, you can find that anywhere.

If you work for a church it's likely because you believe enough in the mission of the church to sacrifice things like time, status, money, and most likely the way you present yourself publicly through things like social media.

Your social media policy can be simple or extensive, but it should align with your church's style and culture as well as your biblical beliefs and overall mission. The idea isn't to control your people and what they say, but to provide them a guide to represent the church and Jesus well. Most of it should be pretty common sense.

Below you'll find a sample Social Media Policy that you may copy and use to develop your own. Take what you want from it, or use it as is.

If it matters, know that this social media policy has been reviewed by competent and licensed attorneys. This specific wording is currently being used by dozens of churches already.

However, I'm not a lawyer and make no guarantees. It

would be wise to have your own counsel as well as your own HR department review and approve the final version you use.

SAMPLE SOCIAL MEDIA POLICY FOR A CHURCH

At Our Church (the "Church"), we know that online social platforms, including blogs, wikis, message boards, video and photo sharing websites, and social networking services, are constantly transforming the way we interact.

We also recognize the importance of the Internet in shaping the public view of our Church. The Church is committed to supporting your right to interact responsibly and knowledgeably on the Internet through blogging and interaction in social media. We want our staff, volunteers, and church attenders to share and learn from others in order to build a valuable online community.

The purpose of these guidelines is two-fold: First, the Church has an aim to protect our interests, including, but not limited to, the privacy of our employees and confidentiality regarding our plans, partners, users, and operations. Second, these guidelines will help you make respectful and appropriate decisions about your work-related interactions with people on the Internet.

Your personal online activity is your business. However, any activity in or outside of work that affects your performance, the performance of others at the Church, or the Church's interests are a proper focus for this Social Media Policy.

You must always assume that your work-related social media activity is visible to the Church as well as current and potential employees, clients, partners, and prospects.

The Church reserves the right to direct its staff to avoid certain subjects and remove inappropriate comments and posts. Our internal policies remain in effect in our workplace.

Guidelines for Discussing Our Church on the Internet

- You are not authorized to speak on behalf of the Church without express permission from your manager.
- If you have permission to discuss the Church and / or our current and potential activities, employees, or partners, please follow these guidelines:
    - Identification: Identify yourself. Include your name, and when appropriate, state your role or title within the Church.
    - Disclaimer: Use a disclaimer that "the views you express on the particular website are yours alone and do not necessarily represent the views of the Church."
    - Proof: Support any statements made online with factual evidence. Use links where appropriate.
- Also, let your manager know about the content you plan to publish. Your manager may want to visit the website to understand your point of view.

Guidelines for Confidential and Proprietary Information

You may not share information that is confidential and proprietary about the Church. This includes, but is not limited to, Church strategy, information about trademarks, upcoming product releases, sales, finances, donation information, discipline or counseling information, and any other information that has not been publicly released by the Church.

The list above is given as example only and does not cover the range of what the Church considers confidential and proprietary. If you have any questions about whether information has been released publicly or any other concerns, please speak with your manager before releasing information that could potentially harm the Church, or our current and potential business interests, employees, partners, or clients.

The Church's logo and trademarks may not be used without explicit permission in writing from the Church. This is to prevent the appearance that you speak for or officially represent the Church. If given permission to use the Church logo, you must use it in accordance to the current Style Guide.

It is fine to quote or retweet others, but you should not attempt to pass off someone else's words, photography, or other information as your own. All copyright, privacy, and other laws that apply offline apply online as well. Always give proper credit to credit your sources when posting a link or information gathered from another source.

Ownership of Social Media Contacts

Any social media contacts, including "followers" or "friends," that are acquired through accounts (including, but not limited to email addresses, blogs, Twitter, Facebook, YouTube, or other social media networks) created on behalf of the Church are the property of the Church.

Transparency and Disclosures

If you have permission to publicly share what a client, partner, or other Church is doing, such as launching a new website or coming out with a new product, you must disclose your relationship to the other party.

Do not discuss a Church or product in social media in exchange for money. If you receive a product or service to review for free, you must disclose it in your post or review.

Respect and Privacy Rights

- Use common sense.
- Follow the rules of the social media sites you use.
- Speak respectfully about the Church and our current or former staff and members.
- Write knowledgeably, accurately, and with appropriate professionalism. Despite disclaimers, your Web interaction can result in members of the public forming opinions about the Church and its employees, partners and interests.
- Refrain from publishing anything that could reflect negatively on the Church's reputation or otherwise embarrass the Church, including posts about drug or alcohol abuse, profanity, off-color or sexual humor, and other inappropriate conduct. Do not use ethnic slurs, personal insults, obscenity, or engage in any conduct that would not otherwise be acceptable in the Church's workplace. Please also show respect for topics that may be considered objectionable or inflammatory.
- Honor the privacy rights of our current staff, members, and partners by seeking their permission before writing about or displaying internal Church information that could be considered a breach of their privacy and confidentiality.
- Ensure that your social networking conduct is consistent with the all policies contained in the Church's Employee Handbook.
- Respect the law, including those laws governing defamation, discrimination, harassment, and copyright and fair use.

Media

Media inquiries for information about our Church and our current and potential products, employees, partners, clients, and competitors should be referred to the Communications Manager. This does not specifically include your opinions, writing, and interviews on topics aside from our Church.

Your Legal Liability

The Church complies with all federal and state laws that apply to our operations and activities. Since you are involved in the Church's operations and activities, you are responsible for understanding and observing these policies.

Note that the breach of privacy and confidentiality, use of copyrighted materials, unfounded or derogatory statements, or misrepresentation may be considered illegal and is not accepted by the Church.

Each person on staff at the Church is personally responsible, and may be legally liable, for the content he or she publishes online. You can be sued for not disclosing your relationship to the Church, or for purposely spreading false information. You can also be sued by Church employees, competitors, and any individual or Church that views your commentary, content, or images as defamatory, pornographic, proprietary, harassing, libelous or creating a hostile work environment. In addition to any legal action, your activity can result in disciplinary action up to and including employment termination.

If you have any questions, please ask the Communications Department or the Human Resources Department for guidance on compliance with the laws.

CHAPTER EIGHT

ENGAGE & ENRAGE

"And the haters gonna hate, hate, hate, hate, hate. Baby, I'm just gonna shake, shake, shake, shake, shake. I shake it off, I shake it off."

- Taylor Swift

In his book *Gift of Fear*, celebrity security consultant Gavin de Becker explains the risks with engaging critics, stalkers, and other detractors.

If you engage with a certain type of people they will only feed on your interaction and become more enraged, never satisfied and never swaying from their negative bias.

In an increasingly hostile world, particularly for Christians, there's more and more temptation to stand our ground or fight back when we experience opposition for our beliefs. However, there is wisdom in backing away and letting the Lord work through other means when it comes to people who have an agenda to distract from our mission.

As Christians, we have a desire for everyone we interact with to meet Jesus and be changed by the gospel, especially our most negative critics. But has anyone ever come to know the Lord by arguing with a Christian over their beliefs?

"For lack of wood the fire goes out, and where there is no whisperer, quarreling ceases. As charcoal to hot embers and wood to fire, so is a quarrelsome man for kindling strife." **- Proverbs 26:20**

ACCEPTING CRITICISM

We must accept criticism and learn from it. We must correct mistakes when they need to be corrected. We must repent when we need to repent. But we cannot become quarrelsome people, or participate in gossip. Doing so would be like throwing more logs on the fire.

Where you'll experience the most criticism is on social media. In order to always handle yourself well as you moderate comments on Facebook, YouTube, and even Twitter, you need to develop a plan and some guidelines to follow. This can be particularly helpful when leaning on volunteers and others to help manage your social media accounts as well.

HANDLING SOCIAL MEDIA COMMENTS

In my experience, there are typically five different types of commenters on social media:

1. those who leave a compliment or express excitement
2. those with genuine and earnest questions
3. those with antagonistic or accusatory questions and statements
4. spammers, or those deliberately leveraging the post to sell something or distribute malware, etc.
5. malicious people who deliberately want to harm your church and seek out your posts to continually distract and bait you and your followers.

For those who leave a compliment, thank them. Followers love interacting with the pages they follow. Like their post, provide a witty reply, or simply thank them for taking the time to comment.

For those with genuine questions, answer them. Feel free to engage to help them with practical questions or theological questions. Usually with theological questions you can point them to resources on your website (sermons and blogs) or even other websites that you trust. You can also reply and tell them to talk to a pastor or deacon after a service, or better yet provide an easy way for them to connect directly with a pastor online.

For spammers, go ahead and delete their comment if you can tell it is spam, if they're asking for money, or if it's telling others to check out another website. You can also block that person from posting again in the future if they continue to abuse your page. If it's someone you recognize, then reach out to them first to let them know the comment was inappropriate and will be deleted. It's usually pretty easy to differentiate between spam and a real person who is just abusing the platform.

For those who are antagonistic commenters, remember the advice from Gavin de Becker: If you engage, you will enrage. These are the type of people who just have to disagree with everything, and a public debate on social media isn't going to change their mind. It will only distract everyone else from the message, and create an awkward experience that won't help your reputation.

Most of the time these types of people are fellow Christians, and maybe even attenders at your church. It's best to ignore their comments and not take the bait. On Facebook, you can hide their comment without deleting it. This way only they and their friends can see it, but it won't appear for anyone else. They'll never know it's hidden, and because no one will be replying to it, they'll likely move on without incident. If you delete it, you risk enraging them for being censored.

Be cautious that you don't appear to ignore anything. You don't want to be seen as replying to only the comments you want to reply to. If you don't want to hide the comment, then reply with something that clearly ends the conversation and moves it offline. Something along the lines of "We understand your concern and welcome the opportunity to chat more about it if you want to message us." This shows publicly that you acknowledged the person, but you aren't going to get into a public debate about it. If they message you, then you can have a private conversation with them. But more often than not, they don't actually want to have a conversation and probably won't message you.

People like that usually aren't looking to learn or get answers to questions, they just want to attack someone or they just want to promote their position. It's usually best to nip antagonistic comments in the bud before they engage debates with your other followers or distract them from the mission of Jesus. If those people honestly want to have a loving conversation then the best place to do that is in person or via email where it isn't public.

If you need to apologize or retract something, go ahead and do it. It's better to apologize publicly than to delete something and pretend it never happened because antagonistic followers will comment on other threads saying that you're hiding something (which you are).

Remember that your social media channels are yours, and they exist to engage with others in a positive and helpful manner. There's nothing wrong with policing your channels and choosing how you want people to use them. Just be honest and candid about it.

On Twitter, you may see people tagging you in mean tweets or harassing your other followers. There's less you can do on Twitter to manage this. The best thing is to ignore anyone who's being antagonistic. Most people following your Twitter account won't even see those tweets unless they do a search. There's also less expectation for interaction on Twitter.

For the final group of people, the malicious people who deliberately want to harm your church, it's best to delete their comments and block them. There is no reasoning with this group. They are like terrorists, and we don't negotiate with terrorists. While we would love for them to become saved and change their ways, that's likely not going to happen through a Facebook debate. These people are wolves, sent to distract you from the mission. Pray for them, and move on.

If people call you out on deleting someone, know why you did it and be prepared to back yourself up. Hopefully you are only deleting and banning as a last resort, so when it happens you'll clearly be able to point out how the person was abusive and how you did your best to love them and meet their needs before having to make a hard decision.

I can't state this clearly enough - blocking should be done as a last resort. These are real human beings you're dealing with online, treat them as such. Think about what you would do if the person were sitting in your worship service on Sunday or walking into your church lobby.

The same rules you have about banning people from your church building should be the same rules you have about banning people from your social media channels.

As Christians, it's also important to always be open to grace and forgiveness. There should be no 'once blocked always blocked' rule. I've seen blocked people beg to be allowed back into the community. Give them a second chance when this occurs. You never know what God is doing in their lives.

CREATE A COMMENT POLICY

A comment policy (or sometimes called an engagement policy) posted to your Facebook page is another great idea to protect you and your church from undue criticism and accusations.

It is simply a set of rules or guidelines that you create which help people know how to engage with your page. It can include reasons why you will delete a comment or ban a user, as well as language and discussions that won't be tolerated, as well as what type of questions are appropriate for Facebook and which type of questions would be better to email.

What you put into the comment policy is up to you. Don't worry if it gets too long, as most people won't actually read the policy before commenting. Rather the existence of the policy is so that people can see you are playing fair and not just haphazardly managing your page.

While no one is legally bound by a comment policy, it can still help build integrity. If people know the expectations up front then they can verify if you're being fair or not if you do have to block someone or remove a post.

Below is a sample comment policy that we have used in the past. Feel free to use the same policy or adapt it as you see fit.

The best place to post this is in the about section of your Facebook page where it can live and easily be linked to. Don't post this as a new post on your page, as it will just get buried over time.

You can also use a comment policy for your other channels, such as Twitter, but you will have to post it on your website and link to it from your bio and posts as needed.

SAMPLE COMMENT POLICY

Thank you for being a part of the community here on our church's Facebook Page.

This page is meant to be a way to keep you informed on various church events and content. It's also an opportunity for us to engage with people who have benefited from our ministry, or who have genuine questions about our church.

The page does have administrators who will do their best to answer reasonable questions or by directing you to existing content that may help you. The administrators also moderate comments and reserve the right to delete any comments or block users who abuse these policies.

Please note that the comments expressed on this page do not necessarily reflect the opinions and position of our church.

In general, the following types of comments are prohibited and will be deleted:

- Hate speech of any kind
- Inappropriate content, including excessively foul language, pornography, etc.
- Self-promotion such as links to personal blogs, websites, etc.
- Requests for donations or money
- Spam of any kind, including reposts of the same comment and/or repeating the same sentiment over and over again
- Promotion of political candidates and policy
- Insults of other commenters or egging other commenters on
- Malicious attacks against church members and leaders

- Anything strange, demanding, obsessive, threatening, etc.
- Anything that infringes on a copyright

If a comment is deleted, consider the deletion a warning. Those who persist in posting comments that are in violation of this policy will be banned from the page.

Things like Facebook are 24/7. However, our administrators are not. Therefore, we ask that, as community members who care about this page, that you do not reply to obvious attempts to bait you into arguments. Please ignore comments in violation of this policy until they can be properly moderated.

...

MODERATING COMMENTS

As you see comments that violate your policy, explain to them your policy through a Facebook message, then delete or hide the comment. If the commenter keeps posting, go ahead and ban them. And of course, use your judgment and discernment. Weigh out the good vs the bad of possible outcomes and just try to be wise. When it comes down to it, comment threads on Facebook hardly ever provide any significant value, so tread lightly and don't stress about moderating. Remember to always have a reason for what you do, and treat each situation on its own. These are real people, not just anonymous commenters.

PRAY FOR YOUR ENEMIES

It can be hard, but don't take hateful comments personally. If your church is preaching the Bible and you're sharing it online, hateful comments can sometimes be a form of spiritual attack, so pray for them and pray for yourself and your church.

Matthew 5:44[8] instructs us to love and pray for those who persecute us. Praying for them gives us the perspective we need to be long suffering and patient before responding or acting out of anger or retaliation. God has the power to change their heart and yours, so you never know what the outcome will be if you stop and pray for people who may not like you.

---

[8] "But I say to you, love your enemies and pray for those who persecute you," - Matthew 5:44 ESV

I also encourage you to always look for ways to improve. Even if someone says something mean hearted, it doesn't mean there isn't truth in their words. Take everything with a grain of salt, but take the time to reflect and ask God if there is anything you need to learn from them. Take what's valuable from it, and leave the rest.

Trust the Holy Spirit to help you discern what is a word from God, wise counsel from a peer, or trash to be ignored.

GRACE AND DONUTS

At the end of the day, we want to be known for grace, not known for enforcing the rules. Keep this in mind when you're dealing with haters, negative commenters, bully reporters, protestors, or even that tough church member.

We got a visit once from the nice fellas at Westboro Baptist Church. I use the words "nice' and "church" pretty loosely here. They are the people known for their protests, the ones where they hold up signs that say, "God hates fags," and "Sinners go to hell." Not necessarily the most biblically sound message nor the most effective medium.

They were kind enough to send out a press release letting people know they planned to protest our church on an upcoming Sunday. In the press release they called our church a whore house, our pastor a false prophet, and claimed that we were all a bunch of blind lemmings for following him. I don't even remember what their issue was with us specifically. They are such a hateful and misguided group that I honestly don't think we put a lot of effort into listening to their concerns.

But we did offer them grace, as well as some donuts and copies of free books on biblical doctrine.

We had these posters printed which welcomed them as they picketed our church entrances.

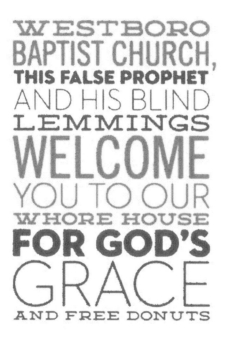

WESTBORO BAPTIST CHURCH, THIS FALSE PROPHET AND HIS BLIND LEMMINGS WELCOME YOU TO OUR WHORE HOUSE FOR GOD'S GRACE AND FREE DONUTS

Sometimes you have to just have a little fun, let people do their thing, and move on. Haters gonna hate. Not everything is worth the panic. Focus on showing people God's grace, and whenever possible offer free donuts.

HOW TO AVOID BURNOUT

With all that said, burnout can still happen. The constant dripping of social media and comments from people who are less than polite. The nasty articles calling your church a cult, and attacking everything you believe in. It can really get to you.

So, what do you do?

There are two things I have found that help with burnout in general, particularly when dealing with a lot of negative feedback.

The first is that whenever you pour yourself out in ministry, you need to take time to be poured back into by Jesus. This means rest and Sabbath, whatever that looks like for you.

For me that means ensuring I have a day off where I don't work at all. Sometimes you can't avoid your boss emailing or calling, or a even a crisis happening on your day off. But that should be the exception and not the norm.

I also moderate my own email and notifications on a daily basis. This means that only certain people make it onto my VIP list. If you're on the list, then I get a notification when you email me. If you're not on the list, then I won't see your message until I check my email next. This way I can block off time to work on something specific, or take a break, and I know that I can safely ignore my phone unless it alerts me.

Little tricks like that can really free up your mind to be able to concentrate on what is important. It is particularly important when I am spending time with my family.

The second is to have your eyes and heart down on the ground. In social media, it can be really easy to view people online as just names, but they're real people who need Jesus. Be active in biblical counseling or prayer ministry if you can, and at least be active in a small group where you can be around other believers.

I joined the baptism team so that I could be in the tub as often as possible. It didn't matter how hard of a week I had, as I would baptize someone I got to hold their hand and hear their story and their profession of faith in Jesus (often for the first time). It gave me the perspective I needed to continue doing what I was doing. Knowing that my hard work throughout the week was paying off in life changing ways was the most satisfying experience.

When you get discouraged or feel off track, that's a great opportunity to learn and grow and focus on our first love, Jesus. Take time to put your head down, get on your knees, and spend more time with Jesus and his word.

Just remember that for every hater out there, there's a lost and hurt person who saw a tweet, came to church and met Jesus for the first time. Find and think about these things[9].

---

[9] "Finally, brothers, whatever is true, whatever is honorable, whatever is just, whatever is pure, whatever is lovely, whatever is commendable, if there is any excellence, if there is anything worthy of praise, think about these things." - Philippians 4:8 ESV

I said earlier that this is war. This is what I mean by that. The more you put yourself out there and interact with others, the more attacks and issues you'll be exposed to. But that's the mission. The alternative is to not engage with people, but that's not church.

Don't let a few haters telling you to quit speak louder than the one guy who says, "you helped me." Keep doing what God wants you to do.

CHAPTER NINE

CONTENT ON CONTENT ON CONTENT

"When you have something at the top, using it as a source for other content is something you have to start thinking about." **- Gary Vaynerchuk, Author and CEO VaynerMedia**

There are enormous opportunities for a church to distribute content inside and outside of your church that will not only help educate and train people, but it can have incredible effects on your reputation and influence.

About a third or more of your social media posts should be content, whether you are sharing your own, or sharing content from other sources. This can help build relationships with others, and it can help with the perception that it's not all about you. Use your channels to not only communicate things you need to communicate, but to also provide value for the people who are following you.

A well thought out content strategy should be an essential piece of your PR plan. Not only because it can be so effective, but because it's just too easy.

You likely have the communications channels already. From social media, to blogs, podcasts, and YouTube, you probably have it all setup but struggle to think of what content to post. You understand you need to post more than just events, but what else is there to post?

Don't stress over creating content. If you open your eyes you'll see that part is already done.

Your church is already producing consistent quality content every single week of the year: your Sunday sermon. Depending on your preacher, you've got 30 to 60 minutes of prime content to work with every week. Let's start there.

4 WAYS TO STRETCH YOUR SUNDAY SERMON

There are four types of content that can easily be extracted from any sermon, and used every week to help your message reach a much larger crowd than who showed up in the pews that week:

- Social Media Quotes
- Blog Posts
- Photos
- Video Clips

That's certainly not everything that can be pulled from a sermon, but it's a place to start. And before you start wincing at all the additional work I'm going to put on your plate, hear me out. It's easier than you think.

SOCIAL MEDIA QUOTES

These are the easiest to collect each week. Assign someone to listen to the sermon on Sunday and write down any pithy quotable phrases that the preacher uses.

Depending on the preacher you should be able to pull anywhere from two to twenty quotes from the sermon. This should give you enough Facebook and Twitter content for the whole week.

Edit the quotes down to 140 characters for Twitter and

schedule them out using Buffer or Hootsuite, or however you schedule social media posts. Pick your top 7 and post one per day, or do multiple a day and use them all up. These work well for Facebook, Twitter, Instagram, or any of the platforms you are using.

This is a great way to help people remember the sermon throughout the week, as they see the quotes pop up in their social media feeds. It can also be a great way to drive more traffic back to your site, especially if you post the sermon online and link to it with each quote.

I have found that many people will share their favorite quotes as a way to show others what their church is all about, and even to invite others to church. It's a lot easier to share one important point, then it is to share the entire sermon.

This doesn't take a lot of time. Chances are you are already listening to the sermon at least once, so it's not a lot of extra effort to write down some quotes as you hear them. You don't have to do it yourself though. This is an excellent task for a volunteer or intern to do.

Some pastors write out pretty detailed sermon notes, and if you're able to get a hold of them you could even pull the quotes out ahead of time, scheduling some to hit on Sunday as the sermon is happening. I personally do this for a handful of churches as a freelance service, so there's plenty of ways to get it done if you can't or don't want to do it on your own.

Go the extra mile and use your favorite apps to create

images out of the quotes. You don't need a graphics design team to get this done. Don't over complicate it. Apps like Over and Adobe Spark easily enable you to create unique and engaging graphics by putting text over designs and photos. Mix up your posts, some with graphics and some just text. Then test what does better with your audience.

BLOG POSTS

The next step is to turn the sermon content into a blog post or two. This is assuming your church utilizes a blog for distributing content on your website (which it should!).

Take the key point of the sermon and condense it down into 300 to 500 words. This is really easy if the preacher included any kind of list or top three points in his sermon.

One of the easiest ways to do this is to take the transcription of the sermon and copy and paste a section into a blog post. Some minor editing and tweaks and it will take you no time at all. If you don't transcribe your sermons already, you can upload an audio or video file to rev.com and they'll transcribe it for $1/minute. $30 to $60 per week is a small price to pay for the convenience, and it provides some great content to put online. Consider including that transcription on your website with the sermon. People like to consume media in different ways. Some prefer audio, some prefer video, and more people than you'd think prefer to read.

A transcription service is also a great way to provide your sermon in multiple languages. For about the same cost you can have the sermon transcribed into Spanish for example. While you may not be able to provide audio or video in Spanish, providing the written sermon is a great step towards reaching a more diverse crowd.

If your church doesn't have a blog already, or building one into your website is going to be a hassle, consider some other options such as posting the blog posts to medium.com or even to your Facebook page as a note. Both have great advantages over your website anyway, as they have the potential to reaching existing audiences that you aren't yet tapping into.

Want to get really crazy? Take those top 7 social media quotes you pulled already, and turn that into another blog post. It could just list them out, or it could be created so that each one is clickable and easily shareable as people read them. Call it the Sermon Social Media Roundup.

Once you start thinking this way, you'll discover you can build content on top of content on top of content. Use the same set of content in multiple different ways, enabling you to reach larger and larger audiences.

PHOTOS

Photos is another easy type of content that you can capture each Sunday, and even throughout the week.

You don't need a fancy camera or a professional photographer on staff to capture photos of the life in your church. Those are great assets to have, but more than likely you've got an iPhone or a similar camera phone in your pocket that is more than capable of taking great photos.

Capture the life in your church. Don't just focus on the preacher or the awesome stage lights and worship band. Take photos of the people, the crowds, and things that show what it's like to participate in your church.

Throughout the week try to capture photos of small groups, weekly events, staff meetings, and other behind the scenes type of content.

This is all content that can be shared on your social media platforms throughout the week, either on its own or linked to the sermon, your blog posts, or other content.

One thing I love to do is to grab an extra phone or iPod Touch and let a trusted volunteer or key member take the phone for a week so that they can capture the church from their unique perspective. Ask them to take photos of their small group, of the events that they attend, photos of the stage but from their particular seat on Sunday. You'll get some unique shots that you would never be able to capture yourself. Whether they use your loaner phone, or used their own, have them submit the photos to you so you can schedule them out. Or if you really trust them, sign them into Instagram and let them post them in real time.

Do you know what I'm going to say next? Just like that Social Media Roundup blog post, consider creating a photo roundup post as well.

We used to publish a post like this every week and it consistently was one of the most popular. All it included was 7 to 10 photos from the week showing what was going on in our church. People ate it up because they wanted to see if they made the cut, and new people checking out our church appreciated the inside look at what the church was really about.

VIDEO CLIPS

This can be a little harder if you don't already have a video team or someone creating sermon videos for you. But posting clips of the sermon each week is a massive opportunity to reach a lot more people with that week's message.

I'm not talking about posting your whole sermon online. That's great and serves a purpose, but it's mostly going to be your own church people watching the sermon online.

By posting shorter clips of the sermon, you open up the potential for key points in the sermon to go viral. It is so much easier to share a three-minute clip of a sermon than it is to post a link to the full service.

People only watch short videos, especially when posted on social media. By pulling two or three clips from the sermon each week, you are creating opportunities for your people to share your content and use it to invite others to church.

Now hopefully you're catching on and you've already thought of my next point. Take those video clips and make yourself a third blog post full of highlights from the sermon. This could easily be combined in the same post as the photo roundup if you wanted to.

That's it. Social media quotes, blog posts, photos, and video clips. And it's all using content that you already produce, and tools you already have in your pocket.

These are all valuable tools that can help grow your church, by using the content you already have. It doesn't take a whole lot of extra effort to produce any of this content. In fact, if you're organized enough, most of it can be done on Sunday shortly after the sermon is preached. By the time you go home for the day, you have an entire week's worth of content scheduled out already.

That frees your week up to be able to engage with people on social media and reply to comments as they consume the content you are posting. It means you don't have to worry about what to post, and can actually use social media as a platform for conversations and community building.

Once you've nailed the process down for these four types of content, start thinking of some other ways you can turn what you already have into more content. Could you create an infographic from the sermon? Maybe not every week, but certainly sometimes. There are a number of templates you can buy to make it easy.

Does the current sermon series deserve its own landing page? Should you start a podcast with the sermon audio? Can the last four sermons be turned into an eBook that you create as a PDF and give way through an email capture form on your site or a Facebook ad? Can some of the photos be turned into funny animated gifs?

Once you get your process down, a single sermon can be stretched out into a dozen or so pieces of content, and the best part is your preacher is doing all the hard work for you already.

They say content is king because it's one of the easiest ways to get people to engage with your church or organization. By providing value to your audience in the form of short, easily consumable content, they can get to know your message better and hopefully share it with others. Don't ignore this massive opportunity you already have before you.

LOOK BEYOND THE SERMON

Once you have your sermon content plan in place, you'll want to look beyond the sermon for ways your church can continue to spread the gospel and reach more people.

Look no further than the Bible sitting on your bookshelf or accessible through the Bible app. This isn't hard. Again, the content is already created for us... we're just in charge of distributing it.

Instead of trying to create content that gets you more likes, or gets you more people in your church, just focus on spreading the Good News and let it work its magic.

The more content you produce that reflects your mission of spreading the gospel, the more you'll be known for just that. Everything you create should point people to Jesus.

You could create weekly YouTube videos where you take biblical questions and provide the answers. You could write daily devotions and distribute them through your blog and Facebook. You could start a podcast where church leaders debate culture and provide biblical context for how Christians should engage with it.

It's too easy these days to distribute content for the church to not be leading the charge. We have the best content to share. It's already produced for us and it will always be relevant and timeless. No one else has that advantage, yet they're lightyears ahead of us already.

Worry about increasing the quality and frequency later. Just start with what you have and don't stop. Because if you aren't sharing content, if you aren't sharing the gospel, then what are you even doing?

CHAPTER TEN

CRISIS PLANNING

"When it comes to crisis communications, if you always focus on building a relationship with your customers, fans and followers, you will always find yourself communicating in the right direction."

– Melissa Agnes, Co-Founder of Agnes + Day

Hopefully by now you've got a hold on your social media plan and content strategy. You see the value in creating content and distributing it to spread the gospel, and how it can help your overall reputation. Your PR plan is coming together and almost feels complete.

But as your exposure is increasing, so is the risk of something going wrong. All your efforts to manage the perception of the church and get your message out to the masses can come crashing down at any moment. Not very encouraging, I know.

That is called a crisis. And you won't be able to control it or avoid it. Just because one has never happened before, doesn't mean it won't ever happen.

It doesn't matter how on the up and up your church is. Every church is susceptible to sin, mistakes, negligence, or even bad weather. Like I said before, if you're doing something right then you'll face persecution and push back. This isn't supposed to be easy. But sometimes it's going to be really hard. You can't plan for any of this, but you can plan for how you'll react and what you'll do if/when something does happen.

That's what crisis management is all about... planning. You must plan ahead so when a crisis hits, you can follow the guidelines and manage the situation in a calm and collected manner. Communication is critical during a crisis - and happens quickly, so the more you plan ahead, the less likely you are to make a mistake or say the wrong thing.

Everything we've covered so far, from building relationships, to social media, is all part of supporting your crisis plan. It's the foundation you've been building so that your crisis plan can be a success. The more stable your reputation is, the better you'll be able to weather a crisis. The stronger your relationships are, the easier you'll be able to navigate through a difficult time.

WHAT IS A CRISIS?

A "crisis" is defined as a problem that can endanger the church's reputation and/or financial position and can occur as the result of a legal, management/employment, advocacy, political, or public relations issue. In short, a crisis is anything that can derail a church or organization from its mission, whether for a short period of time or indefinitely.

It doesn't have to be something your church did wrong. It just has to be something that can affect you and your ability to continue doing church in the most effective way possible. Bad weather can be a crisis. So can the suicide of one of your church members, or your pastor sleeping with someone besides his wife.

We were in a bit of a crisis mode when we realized the shooter at a local Christian school in Seattle was a member of our church. The media never linked the story to us, but we went into crisis mode just in case they did. It would have been devastating had the headlines turned to "Local Church Member Shoots Up School."

You never know what will happen or when it's going to happen, but you can do your best to prepare for almost any scenario.

There are five steps to developing and maintaining an effective Crisis Management Plan that I will cover:

1. Form a Crisis Communications Team
2. Document a Plan
3. Anticipate Common Crisis Scenarios
4. Stay Informed
5. Keep it Updated

FORM A CRISIS TEAM

The Crisis Communications Team should consist of the key players that you will need to convene in the time of a crisis. It is important to decide who these people are now, so you don't waste time debating about it when a crisis hits.

Typically, these are the key decision makers in your church already. The team could include your senior pastor, your executive pastor, elders, board members, HR representatives, and other pastors and ministry leaders. At a larger church, it may include a lawyer, and members of your communications team.

Ideally you want to keep the team small, but include everyone needed to make swift decisions. You can divide the team up into key members and secondary members to make things run more smoothly. The key players may only be the communications director and one executive. If the crisis warrants it, then they decide to bring in the secondary members as needed.

The purpose of this team is to assess a crisis when it occurs, and work together to make quick decisions about what needs to be done, what needs to be said, who should say it, etc.

"Information breeds confidence, silence breeds fear."

- CJ Craig, from The West Wing

Hardly ever should our response to a crisis be to hunker down and wait until it blows over. Believe me when I say that will only work a handful of times before the next one blows the door in.

The goal of your Crisis team is to be able to communicate well the information that needs to be shared at the time, so that you can steer through the storm and keep the ship pointed towards the mission. Say what needs to be said, take the hits you need to take, and get people back on track towards what really matters.

In the next chapter I provide a complete crisis plan that you can copy and use for your church. That plan goes into more details about the Crisis Communications Team and the individual roles of the key players.

Essentially this is the team that executes the tasks outlined in the crisis plan.

DOCUMENT A PLAN

A crisis plan isn't just a loose plan you have in your head. It needs to be written down, rehearsed and constantly adapted. It needs to be something all the key players know about and understand.

When a crisis occurs, you don't have time to suddenly inform your staff and those involved about your crisis plan and how it's going to work. You don't have time to convince them that the plan is good, or debate what should be in it. It needs to already be written, approved, and well known.

As you go through these chapters, start thinking about developing your own crisis plan. By the time you're done reading this book, take our sample plan and start documenting your own right away. Don't put this off for another time. Do it now while it's fresh on your mind. Craft it, pitch it to your bosses and get them to buy into it.

Ideally, you'll update your crisis plan at least quarterly. It needs to be an ever-evolving set of documents. This keeps you fresh and prepared, but also ensures that your plan covers current trends, technology, beliefs and systems of the church, as well as potential threats and situations that may occur as your church grows and adds more people and ministries.

ANTICIPATE COMMON CRISIS SCENARIOS

You won't be able to anticipate and plan for every type of crisis, but you can anticipate, even predict, many of the most common ones.

The idea is to identify the most likely scenarios, and start planning now for what you will do if any of those scenarios become real life.

These are not scenarios that you necessarily think will happen, but are simply things that could happen and therefore they are things we can prepare for. While many are going to be common, each church is going to have a different list of scenarios that are applicable to your context and setting.

For example, a church in Orlando, Florida probably doesn't need to worry about drafting up a plan for what to do if they are hit with a major snow storm.

Start by writing down every possible scenario you can think of that would trigger a crisis at your church.

Some crisis examples are:

• A major service impact issue at one or more local churches due to weather or natural disaster

• A church leader scandal

• Staff or key member death

• An online hack or information leak

• Major website outage affecting donations

• A highly visible or viral campaign against the church

• Accusation of illegal or unethical accounting practices

• Church members forming unsanctioned groups or activities in public that may harm the church's reputation

• A violent crime at a church location

• Picketers or protestors showing up at church

• Bomb threats and other security concerns

• A missing child or kid's ministry incident

• Reporters showing up unannounced at a church event

Keep going until you can't think of any more. Then narrow the list down to the top five that are the most likely to happen at your church.

If you know that you get snowed in every year, then that's something we can plan around. If your church often gets threats, perhaps a security breach is a likely scenario. If you have particular beliefs that you know will be controversial to some, then let's put a plan around how to communicate about it should it stir up some noise.

The next thing you are going to do is write up specific plans for each of these scenarios. You'll pretend that the scenario happened, then walk through each step you should take and start writing it all down.

Not every scenario need a plan prepared ahead of time. Figure out the unique scenarios that may occur at your church, and develop plans for the most likely ones. You may even want to convene your Crisis Communications Team and walk through mock scenarios from time to time. This can be extremely helpful in ensuring everything runs efficiently and smoothly when the real thing happens.

STAY INFORMED

You can't just create a crisis plan, throw it in a binder, and store it on the shelf. You need to be constantly prepared and ready. That means having a pulse on the public perception of your church, the internal perception, current events, political issues, laws that may affect your church or its members, potential threats, security issues, and so much more.

If you think that alone sounds like a full-time job, then you're right. It should be. But chances are you are going to have to juggle it with social media, media relations, and bulletin printing. I suggest planning out your time on a calendar, and ensuring that at least once a day you spend twenty minutes reading articles, searching for your church online, scanning social media, and doing what you can to keep an eye on things.

You'll also want to create a line of communication between

you and your senior leaders so that you aren't the only one judging when a crisis may hit, and so you'll be able to act quickly when it does.

One of the most effective tools I've used to keep your church leaders informed and constantly prepared for a crisis, is delivering a weekly PR Brief.

PREPARING A PR BRIEF

Using various tools and methods the Communications department or PR person for a church should be monitoring news sites, blogs, social media, comment threads, forums, and other internet sites for mentions of the church, its pastors, and topics relevant to the church.

Those mentions can then be vetted, researched, and when necessary, added to a Public Relations Brief that is provided via email to interested parties on a weekly, biweekly, or monthly basis as necessary. Usually this is something that would be communicated between the Communications Director and the Senior Leaders or Lead Pastor in order to keep them informed.

This concept is very similar to what the President of the United States receives on a daily basis, called the President's Daily Brief or PDB. The more informed you are about your surroundings and the public's perception, the more you can anticipate when a crisis may hit. Sometimes this knowledge alone is enough to help you avoid the crisis, but if it does hit you'll have more time to prepare.

While daily may be a bit excessive, to maintain organized communication between the Communications Team and the Senior Leaders of the church, I recommend preparing a weekly PR Brief which covers the following information:

- **New Issues:** situations that the Senior Leaders should be aware of
- **Status of Issues in Progress:** ongoing issues that the Senior Leaders are already aware of, and the status of our actions
- **Potential Issues:** issues that may or may not come to realization but that are being monitored and prepared for by the Communications Director
- **Internal Issues:** issues regarding staff, pastors, deacons or members that the Senior Leaders needs to be aware of
- **Issues Worth a Mention:** issues that don't require action or active monitoring but Senior Leaders should be aware of
- **Wins:** public relations items that have had a positive external or internal impact

Each item mentioned in the brief should also include recommended actions from the Communications Director. While the decision making may be left to your senior leaders, the Communications Director should work as an informed advisor who can make recommendations based on what they are seeing and hearing.

RATING SYSTEM

In the PR Brief, new issues can be rated 1-5 concerning their severity and action needed. This helps prioritize what needs to happen first, and makes the weekly brief easier and quicker to read.

- **High Urgency:** Action is needed and this issue should be addressed immediately.
- **High Risk:** This issue should be addressed within 24-48 hours and may need immediate action.
- **Medium Risk:** This issue may or may not require immediate action but should be addressed this week.
- **Low Risk:** Problem can be resolved with current resources, does not require immediate action.
- **FYI:** This is information you need to know. No immediate action is required.

KEEP YOUR PLAN UPDATED

Lastly, you'll want to keep your Crisis Plan updated. You can't just write it up and stick it on a shelf. It will become a living document that you should update monthly.

Schedule time on your calendar, once per month, to look through the crisis plan and make updates. Do any contacts need to be updated? Were there staff changes or phone numbers that changed?

Are there new scenarios that can be added based on the way your church has grown, or how things in culture have progressed? Sometimes a law will pass in your area that may affect your church. Update the plan on how you'll respond if it becomes an issue.

I also suggest on a quarterly basis holding a staff meeting where you remind everyone of your crisis procedures, and update their individual versions of the plan. You may also need to update anything that has been added to the employee handbook.

One thing we did to keep people fresh and aware was to hold monthly staff training webinars. Each month a different team lead would host a webinar via video conference on their area of expertise. One month it was training on social media best practices, the next it was HR updates.

Work in a webinar on crisis management and make sure people know what to do if they are contacted by someone from the press, or what to do if a camera crew shows up at church unannounced. The more you talk about it, the more people will be prepared and won't panic if something happens.

CHAPTER ELEVEN

READY-TO-USE CRISIS PLAN

"By the time you hear the thunder,

it's too late to build the ark."

- Unknown

A crisis is something you hope you'll never have to face, and you probably work hard to avoid being in the negative spotlight. But in the world we live in today, no church is immune to an attack by our enemy or the sinful behavior of our people. It is best to be prepared so you know how and why you will communicate what you want to say (and not say) during those moments.

To get you started, I have included a complete crisis communications plan that you may copy and use at your church or organization. I've included it here so you can see what's in it, but you can also download a free copy at churchprbook.com/bookperks.

Keep in mind that this plan was originally developed for a large megachurch with multiple locations and a high profile senior pastor. It has changed over many years of using it in real crisis scenarios at churches big and small.

This version has been edited to be more generic, in order to give you a base to use as you develop your own Crisis Communications Plan.

Please feel free to take and copy the entire plan and make it your own. Change the wording and phrasing to match your context and needs, or use it as is.

Throughout the plan I refer to the primary contact and keeper of the plan as the "Communications Director." At your church, this person may be called something else, perhaps a Communications Manager, PR Manager, Marketing Manager, or the role may be filled by your Executive Pastor, Worship Pastor, or someone else. Change the field to match your church's unique staffing structure.

What matters most here is that a single individual or position within your church is tasked with ownership and maintenance of this plan.

I also refer a lot to "Senior Leaders." The terminology used here can also vary from church to church, so replace this with what works best for you. This is referring to your Lead or Senior Pastor. In some cases, there may be a team of senior officials at your church. Who makes the final decision in your church?

These documents are by no means all inclusive, but they should be enough for any size church or organization to start a plan of their own. I hope what I've developed here will help take some of the obstacles away for you as you prepare and plan for the future of your church.

I've included this sample plan on the following pages so you can see what is included, but be sure to download your own copy, which you are free to use and edit, at churchprbook.com/bookperks. I've also included additional documents such as Likeness Release Form, the sample Social Media Comment Policy, and more.

WHAT'S INCLUDED?

The sample crisis plan includes the following assets:

CHURCH CRISIS COMMUNICATIONS PLAN

This is the master plan which you must keep updated and maintain monthly. It includes how to pro-actively prepare for a crisis, and walks you through step by step what to do during and after a crisis. It is best to make copies of this plan and keep it in binders or on an online intranet so that department heads and ministry leaders can easily access it and refer to it as needed. You will update this asset several times a year.

CRISIS MANAGEMENT POLICIES & PROCEDURES

This document contains policies and procedures that you may enter into your employee handbook or use to develop a job description for your Communications Director. These policies and procedures should guide your philosophy behind how you wish to respond to any crisis. Adapt it as needed to fit your needs.

ACTIVE CRISIS WORKSHEET

This is a simple worksheet to fill out during a crisis that will help you gather all the important information needed to effectively manage the crisis. This helps keep your entire team on the same page, and by having these questions written down ahead of time ensures you don't miss a step during a crisis.

CRISIS CHECKLIST

This is a one page checklist of questions the Communications Director should ask and fill out at the start of a new crisis. Having this developed and accessible beforehand helps ensure you are asking and answering the right questions during a crisis, when your head may not be the clearest and you certainly don't have the time.

LOCAL CAMPUS ONE SHEET

If your church has multiple campuses or locations, this one sheet can be helpful to distribute to each campus so they know what their role is if a crisis situation presents itself locally at their location. For example, it explains what to do when press and media show up on a Sunday at their location.

...

CHURCH CRISIS COMMUNICATIONS PLAN

OVERVIEW

The purpose of this document is to pro-actively layout a plan for directing communications during a crisis, so that we are able to act swiftly and consistently in a way that reflects the mission and work of the church and honors God.

While this plan includes step by step instructions to follow during a crisis, it is imperative to the success of this plan that it be read and understood in its entirety by all who may be involved in the execution of this plan should a crisis arise.

GOAL OF THIS PLAN

This plan will serve as a comprehensive guide in the event of a communications crisis and will enable our teams to respond to the crisis in a timely, effective, well-considered, sensitive way that is appropriate to the severity of the crisis.

This plan will also strive to ensure that issues are not escalated inappropriately in situations which appear to be a crisis but in fact are not.

INTENDED RECIPIENTS OF THIS PLAN

List the recipients or groups of recipients who will receive a copy of the plan (such as ministry teams, pastors, all staff, connection volunteers, social media volunteers, etc.)

ASSUMPTIONS MADE WITH REGARD TO THIS PLAN

• You know how to deal positively with media representatives in accordance with this document.

• You will respond in a timely manner to all correspondence with regard to this plan, or you will appoint someone to do so on your behalf.

• You understand the overall position and voice of the church on key issues.

• You have a clear understanding of whether or not you are authorized to speak on behalf of the church and/or its leaders and in which medium (broadcast, print, online, etc.) this authorization applies.

KEY CONTACTS

List the name, position, phone number, and email address of every person in your organization who may need to be contacted in the event of a crisis. This usually includes your communications team members, senior leaders, board members, and any other decision makers. Having this list printed in your plan and continually updated helps save time during a crisis.

KNOWN LOCAL NEWS CONTACTS

You should also include a list of known media contacts that you can rely on to get information out during a crisis.

BEFORE A CRISIS

MAINTENANCE OF THIS PLAN AND RELATED ASSETS

This plan and the assets that support this plan will be revised and updated at regular intervals to make sure that all information is current when it is needed. Content will undergo a light review monthly and a deep review quarterly.

Content may also be updated after a self-assessment of the Communications Team reveals areas where this plan can be improved upon.

TEAM STRUCTURE AND FLOW OF INFORMATION

The Communications Director is the primary person on the Communications Team who has the authority to call this plan into action. The Communications Director may appoint someone to carry this authority in his absence. The Senior Pastor may also call this plan into action.

Information and communications that occur as a result of this plan must be coordinated by the Communications Director unless he or she delegates that authority.

RECOGNIZING A COMMUNICATIONS CRISIS

A "crisis" is defined as a problem that can endanger the church's reputation and/or financial position and can occur as the result of a legal, management/employment, advocacy, political, or public relations issue.

A crisis can be anything from bad weather shutting down a church service, to a pastor being accused of moral failure. An event is a communications crisis if it is deemed so by the Communications Director or his approved substitute, or by Senior Leadership.

In order for an event to be deemed a communications crisis, the responsibility for mitigating the communications crisis must clearly fall within the goals and the scope of the church. If a communications crisis is deemed to be active then this plan will go into effect.

Remember that many events deemed as a communications crisis are not "PR problems" at their core; they are actual conflicts that involve actual people.

DURING A CRISIS

ESSENTIAL ACTION ITEMS DURING A CRISIS

In the event of a communications crisis, take these steps immediately:

PAUSE AND PRAY

Take a moment to ask for God's direction and discernment.

INFORM LAW ENFORCEMENT

If there is any indication that illegal activity was conducted by any party, anyone acting under the scope of this plan must contact law enforcement immediately with the relevant details.

If you are trying to decide whether or not to contact law enforcement, the answer is yes.

The same is true if you are in the position to suggest that someone else contact law enforcement about a possible crime. The church is not in the business of protecting people from a legal investigation no matter who they are or what their affiliation with the church is.

INFORM THE PRIMARY CONTACT

The Communications Director must be informed immediately of any activities undertaken as relates to this plan.

DISABLE LOGIN ACCESS

If a crisis involves an individual who has login access to internal or external church communications platforms and/or file management systems, such as CMS and email, all attempts should be made to immediately disable those logins. Logins are a privilege extended by the church, not the right of an individual, and they can be restored at a later time.

PROTECT THE IDENTITY OF MINORS

If there is an individual under the age of 18 involved in a crisis, that individual's identity, likeness, location, age and all other related information should be secured so that it cannot be accessed by anyone who is not in receipt of this plan document. All reasonable action should be taken to this end regardless of what role the underage individual is playing within the crisis. The minor's parents and/or guardians should be involved as soon as possible.

CONVENE THE CRISIS COMMUNICATIONS TEAM

The individual who activates the plan is the Team Director. Ideally this person is the Communications Director and keeper of this plan. In certain crisis scenarios, it may make sense for the Communications Director to assign someone else as the Team Director, particularly if the crisis directly affects or involves the Communications Director or their family.

The first order of business for the Team Director is to

convene the entire team.

The team will then select a Spokesperson and an Internal Communications Manager. Often these will be the same person, but dividing these roles up may be appropriate in certain scenarios.

The Spokesperson will be the primary contact for all media inquiries including press conferences, press interviews and internal announcements. The Spokesperson must also approve any copy or content that is distributed through online media and social networks.

The Internal Communications Manager (ICM) will assist the Director and is primarily responsible for:

- Ensuring that this plan is executed
- Ensuring that the team has the most current and developing information at all times
- Seeing that the decisions of the Director and of the team are carried out appropriately

After the roles are appointed, the team will complete the Active Crisis Worksheet.

INTERNAL TEAM COMMUNICATIONS

The primary method of team communication during a crisis should be on email. All members of the Crisis Communications Team mentioned on the worksheet below should be copied on all communications.

Email is the easiest and most universal form of communication and is not dependent on any one app or device. This ensures everyone you may need to involve can be easily communicated with.

It is important to direct all communications outside of in-person meetings through email so that nothing is forgotten and there is a record of all communication. If needed, all other email except for those coming from the Crisis Communications Team can be avoided during an active crisis.

ACTIVE CRISIS WORKSHEET

Use this sheet to gather pertinent information during a crisis.

1. What name will we give this communications crisis for internal use?

2. What other resources from the Crisis Communications Team folder will be utilized to handle this event?

3. Who is the Team Director, the Spokesperson and the Internal Communications Manager?

4. Who else is on the team and needs to be included in all communications?

5. What is the nature of the crisis and where is it being played out?

6. Rate the need to disseminate a public response:
- Immediate
- Within the day
- Within two or more days
- Not immediate or evolving with the event

Use this chart to determine messaging for each key audience that needs to be addressed regarding the crisis, including how they will be messaged and what supporting facts should be utilized.

Audience	Key Message	Supporting Facts	Comm Channels

Use this chart to determine which key elements of the crisis need monitoring and make assignments.

Requires Monitoring	Who is Monitoring

7. What are the sources of the content needed in order to respond to this event? (an individual, a specific Crisis Scenario Plan, etc.)

8. If applicable, where should public media be directed to find the most updated information about the event?

9. If applicable, where should internal audiences be directed to find the most updated information about the event?

10. Are there any internal weaknesses or conflicts of interest that the team must address?

11. Do we need a translator in order to respond adequately to this crisis?

12. If law enforcement is involved in this crisis, is the team informed about their needs? And, how will we ensure that the team is fully cooperative?

13. Is there anyone for whom we need to attempt securing a Likeness Release Form?

14. What date and time should the entire team convene again to collaborate on this event?

CRISIS CHECKLIST

What is the nature of this communications event?

Who needs to be involved in working this event?

What tasks or roles are assigned to me for completion?

Who is the Internal Communications Manager managing this event?

Do I need to prepare for interviews?

What surprises should I prepare for?

Is there anything unique about this event to be mindful of?

How might this event impact or influence other active communications events?

Should I communicate up the chain about this and what should I say?

Is this event going to expand from one media format to another?

Do I need to communicate anything to the content or web teams?

Are online and real-world security and privacy threats being mitigated?

Are local church teams going to have what they need?

AFTER A CRISIS

The Team Director will determine when the communications crisis is over. Within a few days of that time, the Communications Crisis Team will assemble for an evaluation and complete the following worksheet.

EVALUATION WORKSHEET

What worked well?

What could have gone better?

Were the messages received and interpreted in the way we intended?

Did the messages elicit the expected response?

Did the channels of communication we use worked as we expected?

Did we effectively monitor the situation and were we able to adapt our response as needed?

How can we modify this plan or related resources to improve it?

What would we do differently regarding a future, similar communications crisis?

Were there any specific issues that came up which should be reported to another part of the organization? (Example: A behavior by a staff member during the crisis.)

CHURCH CRISIS MANAGEMENT POLICY

The following are crisis management policies you may adopt for your church and place in your employee handbook, bylaws, or any other necessary document.

Our church is committed to taking a biblical and preemptive approach to public relations crises, using disclosure whenever possible as the preferred strategy for preventing or minimizing public relations crises.

A "crisis" is defined as a problem that can endanger the church's reputation and/or financial position and can occur as the result of a legal, management/employment, advocacy, political, or public relations issue.

A crisis can take one of two forms: building over time or all of a sudden. During a crisis, both internal and external messages must be strategically written and consistently delivered to minimize a negative public relations crisis or the outflow of inaccurate or incomplete information. It is important to control the distribution of messages and documents from the Church so that accurate and non-contradictory messages are shared.

With the foregoing purpose in mind, it shall be the policy of our church that:

- All media interviews and inquiries at any time are to be coordinated through the Communications Director.
- Generally, the principal spokesperson(s) for the church is the Communications Director. During times of a crisis communication, no person shall be authorized to speak to the news media in a crisis without prior clearance from the Communications Director. The Communications Director may direct specific staff members to serve as the media contacts for specific projects, issues or media releases.
- The Communications Director shall be responsible for developing and implementing the Church's crisis communication strategies. These strategies will be circulated and reviewed annually by the Board. The final approval of these strategies shall be subject to the consent of the Senior Leaders.

CRISIS MONITORING & PREVENTION

The Communications Director shall be responsible for monitoring local, state, and national news coverage issues, blogs, and social media, advising the Senior Leaders of issues and/or trends that might lead to negative stories or opportunities for the church to support public dialogue on issues central to its work and mission.

The Communications Director will maintain regular contact with the Senior Leaders and shall be responsible for advising the when internal or external issues or developments appear likely to lead to public relations problems.

Similarly, the Senior Leaders will regularly notify the Communications Director of internal developments that may escalate into public relations crises.

CRISIS RESPONSE PROCEDURES

When crises erupt, the Communications Director, under the leadership of the Senior Leaders, shall be responsible for gathering and verifying information about the crisis, assessing the severity of the crisis, and developing strategies to address the crises, such as how information is to be released, who should speak for the church, and who is to be notified.

The Communications Director will reach out to media consultants and legal counsel, as appropriate, work out logistical details of releasing information, and distribute verified information as quickly as possible to internal and external audiences, depending on the type of crisis, as outlined below.

TYPES OF CRISES

1. Foreseeable Crises
    • Crisis assessment: The Communications Director will be notified immediately of an emerging crisis by the Senior Leaders and will work with them to determine who should be involved in the crisis team.
    • Formation of a crisis team: The crisis team will

gather as many details as possible, recommend strategies for internal and external communication, potential involvement of legal counsel or external communications consulting and select an appropriate spokesperson(s). The Senior Leaders have final approval of the recommendations. The crisis team serves as long as the Senior Leaders deem necessary.

2. Sudden Crises

- Immediate action: When the sudden occurrence of a severe crisis precludes convening a crisis team, the Communications Director will draft and implement a strategy immediately upon approval of the Senior Leaders.

- After implementing a "first-wave" communication strategy, under the direction of the Executive Team, the Communications Director will convene the crisis team to develop ongoing strategy.

ESTABLISHING CLEAR LINES OF COMMUNICATION

The Communications Director will be authorized to gather and verify information in a crisis, and will be the only person authorized to release information.

1. Releasing Information Internally

- Upon approval of the Senior Leaders, the Communications Director will inform church elders, staff, and members (in that order) of the crises in any appropriate manner before details are released externally.

2. Releasing Information Externally

• After internal notifications, under leadership of the Senior Leaders, the Communications Director will work with the crisis team to prepare a briefing sheet providing instructions to the chosen spokesperson(s) as to how to handle questions regarding the crisis.

• When deemed appropriate by the Senior Leaders the Communications Director will work to supply verifiable details to the news media as rapidly as possible. All statements and information to be distributed to the media shall first be reviewed and approved by the Senior Leaders.

• After releasing information, the Communications Director will monitor the news coverage and quickly correct any errors that are made, conduct an assessment of the lessons learned, and propose any new guidelines for the next crisis to the Senior Leaders.

3. Communicating With the Board

• During a Crisis:

• During a crisis the Senior Leaders and Communications Director will conduct planning and strategy on a regular basis, with the expectation that they will provide at the conclusion of the crisis an evaluation and follow-up report to the Board.

• Where Disqualifying Charges are Made

• In the event the crisis involves disqualifying charges being made about any one of the Senior

Leaders, the Communications Director will communicate and report directly to the Board for oversight and planning during the crisis.

EVALUATION AND FOLLOW-UP

The Communications Director will document the news coverage surrounding a crisis, including social media, wire stories, newspaper articles, radio, and television broadcasts.

When the crisis is past, the Communications team will supply the Crisis Team and Senior Leaders with a summary of news coverage, in addition to a full evaluation and follow-up report about the crisis. This report will then be provided to the Board.

LOCAL CAMPUS CRISIS PLAN

For use with multi-campus churches.

Know that at your local church, you are not responsible for dealing in depth with the press. However, you should be ready to communicate with them on a cursory basis at any given time.

The press includes TV, radio and print reporters, high profile bloggers, news personalities and any agents of the same.

Typically, you'll have notice when members of the press want to visit a church event, however if they are responding to a live event such as a protest then they may show up unannounced.

COORDINATING PRESS INTERVIEWS

If you know in advance that someone from the media will be at church or an event, please coordinate that with the Communications Director beforehand. Please do not conduct any interview or speak with any member of the press without coordinating with the Communications Director first.

UNANNOUNCED INTERVIEWS

If press shows up unannounced on a Sunday or at a mid-week event:

- A senior leader should greet them and thank them for coming. Do not tell them to go away.

- Inform them that you don't want to disrupt Sunday services, and that our Communications Director would be happy to speak with them over the phone to coordinate whatever they need.

- Get their name, company name, and phone number (ask for a card or to see their credentials).

- Give them the contact information for the Communications Director.

- Let them know that they may perform journalism activities outside, but that doing so inside will disrupt services and cannot be permitted.

Immediately inform the Communications Director about the event and relay all pertinent information such as the name and contact info of the reporter.

We do not hold you responsible for dealing with the press or any unplanned communications event, and we are here to help you. When you are dealing with the press, remember to be polite, professional and helpful. Do not say "no comment" or offer anything "off the record". Simply refer them to the Communications Director.

CHAPTER TWELVE

GO JUMP OFF A CLIFF

"To be prepared for war is one of the most effective means of preserving peace." **- George Washington**

One of my favorite TV shows is The West Wing. I didn't watch it when it was on, but recently I viewed the whole series on Netflix and loved it. While I thought it would be too much about politics, it actually stays pretty moderate and the story centers mostly around the communications team at the White House. There's a lot that can be learned from watching one of the most influential communications teams in the world, even if it's a fictional one.

One of the best episodes is called "Third Day Story" in season six. In the episode, Chief of Staff Leo McGarry suffers a heart attack and can no longer fulfill his duties for the White House. As he and the President, Jed Bartlett (played by Martin Sheen), reminisce about their past six years together, Leo asks the President, "You remember what you told me when you offered me the job?"

The President nods and replies, "I need you to jump off a cliff."

In the next scene, we see the President pull aside his press secretary, C.J. Cregg, and he says, "C.J., I need you to do something for me... Jump off a cliff." While that probably sounded odd to C.J. we quickly discover he was promoting her as the new Chief of Staff to replace Leo McGarry.

I share this story because it's time for you to jump off a cliff.

You've read this far. There's so much more I can share with you that would help your church reach the next level when it comes to communicating well and reaching a larger audience.

And so much more I can share about protecting your church and preparing for a crisis. But that's all content for another time. It's time for you to get to work.

I've given you the basic tools you need to survive in this ever-changing, but increasingly hostile climate, as well as some tools to help you thrive and take your communications to the next level.

Even though I feel like I've only just brushed the surface, I hope these tips have been practical enough for you to get started working on a PR strategy for your church.

I've walked you through what PR is, and why your church should care. I've shown you the power of working with the press, the power of utilizing social media as your biggest opportunity to reach the world and engage with your community. You've seen the value in creating and distributing content, and how easy it is to create with the resources you already have. And I've helped you plan for a crisis, so you can be prepared when things get tough.

Now it's time to put it all into action. The mission is too important for you to ignore what's already happening around you, and think you can survive doing it the way you've always done it. I have no more patience for churches who choose to be naive or are too lazy or scared to do things differently than they've done for the past 200 years.

I know you think your church is small. I know you're under staffed and under resourced. I know you're doing a great job already. But better is still possible. We have a lot of work to do to get the church up to speed.

Everything I've shared in this book is easy to do and already uses the tools that you have in front of you. Nothing I described takes a large team or expensive equipment. Use the tools you have already and do the best you can with it before worrying about your next hire or that expensive camera.

If you feel alone or you're not empowered to make the changes you know you need to make, then hand this book to your pastor. When he's done reading it, ask him if he's ready to jump off a cliff with you. (Make sure he's actually read it first, otherwise that may not go over so well.)

My job here is done. The church has the best story to tell, and you have the tools in front of you to be the best at telling it. Now it's time for you to get out there and continue to boldly proclaim the Good News of Jesus Christ, prepared for whatever may get in your way.

DOWNLOAD FREE BOOK PERKS

Download the complete crisis plan, social media policy, and many other helpful resources for FREE at

churchprbook.com/bookperks

Available for free with this book purchase.

JUSTIN DEAN

ABOUT THE AUTHOR

Justin Dean is a church communications advisor and entrepreneur.

He served in senior marketing roles in the corporate startup world for over a decade before joining Mars Hill Church in Seattle as the Communications Director in 2011. He oversaw all social media, content, editorial, communications, and public relations for the growing megachurch until they ultimately closed their doors for good at the end of 2014.

He is now the co-founder of That Church Conference, helping digital communicators tell the best story the church has to tell through conferences, workshops, and online resources (learn more at thatcc.com).

When he's not helping churches, Justin can often be found on the lake or eating tacos with his wife and four kids. You can contact Justin on Twitter @justinjdean or go to justinjdean.com for more info.

ACKNOWLEDGEMENTS

I am incredibly grateful to my wife Heidi, and my adorable children, Dylan, Evelyn, Ellie, and Jake, for sacrificing so much, not only as I wrote this book, but throughout the years as we have continued to serve the church. It's a wonderful thing to have a family that's on mission.

I'm thankful for the support of godly men who have spoken into my life over the years, namely Mark Driscoll, Sutton Turner, and Greg Laurie. It has been an honor to serve in the trenches with these men.

Thank you to the friends who have risked their own reputations to lift mine up and encourage me to continue doing what God has called me to do: Van Baird, Tim Schraeder, Dave Adamson, Matt McKee, Chris Dunagan, Ashley Williams, Kem Meyer, Carrie Kintz, Justin Brackett, Carey Nieuwhof, Nils Smith, Greg Laurie, Brendan Stark, Paul Briney, Stephen Posey, Daniel Irmler, Jonathan Malm, Andy Girton, Jesse Wisnewski, Phil Bowdle, Jim Tinsley, and many others. Also to every stranger who has listened to a podcast or read an article and took the time to email or DM me... your words of encouragement have saved me from giving up countless times.

And thank *you*! I appreciate you taking the time to read this book. I truly hope it is helpful for you and your ministry.

ADDITIONAL NOTES

Portions of this book were taken from Social Media Guide for Churches (2015) by Justin Dean and Corrin Bauer.

Other publications mentioned in this book and recommended by the author:

• So You've Been Publicly Shamed by Jon Ronson (Riverhead Books, 2015)

• Less Chaos. Less Noise. by Kem Meyer (2016)

• A Call to Resurgence: Will Christianity Have a Funeral or a Future? by Mark Driscoll (Tyndale, 2013)

• The Gift of Fear: And Other Survival Signals That Protect Us from Violence by Gavin de Beker (Dell, 1998)

• Trust Me, I'm Lying: Confessions of a Media Manipulator by Ryan Holiday (Portfolio, 2013)

76371249R00125

Made in the USA
Columbia, SC
07 September 2017